The Kahn Report On Sexual Preferences

The Kahn Report On Sexual Preferences

Sandra S. Kahn, M.A.
with Jean Davis, Ph.D.

W. H. ALLEN • LONDON
A Howard & Wyndham Company
1981

For information, write: St. Martin's Press,
175 Fifth Avenue, New York, N.Y. 10010
Manufactured in the United States of America

Printed and bound in the United States of America
for the Publishers, W.H. Allen & Co. Ltd,
44 Hill Street, London W1X 8LB

ISBN 0 491 02605 6

To Brenda Clorfene Solomon, M.D.
with deepest gratitude

Sex is difficult; yes. But they are difficult things with which we have been charged. . . . If you only recognize this and manage, out of yourself, out of your *own* nature and ways, out of your *own* experience and childhood and strength to achieve a relation to sex wholly your own (*not* influenced by convention and custom), then you need no longer be afraid of losing yourself and becoming unworthy of your best possession.

RILKE, *Letters on Love*

Contents

Introduction

HAVING been married for twelve years, both Marsha and Fred knew that, since tonight was Friday and Johnny Carson had just finished his monologue on the "Tonight" show, they would make love.

As Marsha crawled into bed, Fred asked her, as he had asked her every Friday night for as long as Marsha cared to remember, if she was "in the mood." Marsha replied with a pleasant smile and removed her nightgown. She then turned over flat on her back. Fred immediately placed his hand on one of Marsha's breasts and began to massage the nipple vigorously. Marsha allowed this for as long as she could before the painful irritation of the nipple caused her to move his hand away. She now knew that he would take this cue to put his mouth on the other nipple and begin to suck. She wished he would be more gentle.

Marsha hoped that she could become more aroused so that when Fred moved his hand to her vagina she would be wet for him. Perhaps then, as almost never happened, his fingers would slide smoothly over her clitoris instead of commencing the harsh rubbing she knew she would shortly be feeling. Marsha yearned for the natural wetness that she felt when she read Rosemary Rogers's novels or when she fantasized and masturbated. Marsha had read that some women loved to have their partner rub hard on their clitoris, but she had always experienced more discomfort than pleasure when Fred did that to her.

For Fred's pleasure, Marsha felt some obligation to begin to rub his penis, since he did try to arouse her. She took the hardened penis into her hand and began to push up and down. Fred uttered a sigh of pleasure, but he was actually thinking how he would like Marsha to use her mouth instead of merely grasping and manipulating his penis by hand. Her grip was often too close and tight and she was rarely sensitive to the rhythms of his erection.

Once Fred had tried to gradually move Marsha's head toward his penis, but she seemed to resist doing that. Marsha had actually always wanted to try oral sex, but could not bear talking about it. She needed more encouragement, and she had been willing the one time Fred had tried to get her to put her mouth on his penis, but he had stopped abruptly, for some reason or other. Now, after pushing her hand up and down on Fred's penis, Marsha got ready for Fred to enter her by opening her legs.

She had often longed for him to take this opportunity to kiss her entire body, even perhaps use his tongue to stimulate various parts of her body so that she would become increasingly aroused. Then Fred would not have to rely on the small jar of Vaseline he kept in the first drawer of his bedside table.

When Fred saw Marsha open her legs, he simply assumed she was ready. It was difficult for Marsha to become lubricated, as he supposed it was difficult for most women. Fred smoothed a fingertip of Vaseline on his penis before entering her. He wished that there were a way for Marsha to abandon herself more to passion, to really come to the point of begging him to enter her, but wives weren't like that.

Marsha wanted to tell Fred that she was not ready, wanted to ask him to take longer in preparing and exciting them both. Ever since the beginning of their marriage Fred had always taken the aggressive role in their sex life. She did not want to risk hurting his feelings now by taking over and making suggestions.

For some time Fred had felt that Marsha could be more interesting if she would express herself more in bed. He wanted to feel that she really loved having sex with him and that she would suddenly initiate new ways, for a change, such as getting on top of him. Marsha never did things like that.

Marsha closed her eyes and waited for Fred's penis to enter her. She knew it would not be long before she would feel his body tense, shudder, and then collapse, as, in fact it did, when Fred, moving in and out of Marsha, had a fleeting rememberance of the picture of a nude woman he kept in his desk at the office and, at that moment, ejaculated inside his wife.

Before getting up to take his shower, Fred asked Marsha, "Hon, did you come?" Marsha answered, as she had answered for hundreds of Friday nights, "Yes, Fred."

If this situation sounds familiar to you, or if you have ever wondered what it would be like to share a fantasy or a secret desire with a partner, or if you or your partner ever wanted to suggest new and different forms of sexual activity, then you need this book. It can show you how to find out what sexual activities you prefer to perform, how to know what other potential sex partners might enjoy, and how to communicate about them so that you need not have another sexual encounter that is confusing, frustrating, and unsatisfying.

As adult men and women, we have been blinded by sexual enlightenment. Onslaughts of information about sex are upon us all the time. This outpouring of material on a subject that has for decades been treated by silence is confusing to many men and women.

At every bookstore we find a smorgasbord of titillating items on sex. In the last few years, the emphasis has been on popularized material concerning female sexuality. We are overwhelmed with instructions and techniques regarding female fantasy, vaginal/clitoral orgasm, self-stimulation, lesbianism, adultery, and positions for intercourse ad infinitum.

Unfortunately, this emphasis on techniques for sexual satisfaction and success has done little to educate us on the process of communication between the sexes. Much of this material has caused befuddlement and mystification. Men and women find themselves reading book after book and asking, "Where do I fit in?" or, "What's in this for me?"

One book may advise a woman to take the role of aggressor in all sexual encounters, another might applaud the virtues of various lovers, and a third insist that a woman depend only upon herself for true satisfaction. Women who read these books are overwhelmed with the number of options they find available to them. Men who read these books begin to wonder if their real competition lies in other men, other women, animals, or electric vibrators.

Almost all of us, given the conditions of our upbringing and the pressures of peers and culture, have experienced some shyness and difficulty in being openly honest and expressive about our sexual needs, wants, and preferences. Now, with an entire body of literature that tells us which specific techniques to use in what specific situations, people are feeling even more confused.

That is why I wanted to write this book about sexual attitudes and sexual preferences. It is a book that can help men and women learn more about what sexual activities each sex prefers and how to communicate and express these preferences to each other. It is a book that attempts to explain why men and women have trouble telling one another what sexual activities they enjoy. It is a book that will increase your knowledge of the opposite sex, make you more comfortable in talking about your own preferences in sexual activities, and help you achieve a more mutually satisfying sex life with your partner.

The reasons for my writing the book go back some ten years in my own personal history. After five years of marriage and the birth of one son, I had been living a fairly comfortable conventional suburban life. I was, up to this point, happy in my role of homemaker, wife, and mother. I then gave birth to my daughter. When this new female life reached the age of five or six months, I began to feel a certain restlessness, a vague sense of internal stirrings that I could not define or identify. My husband, who knows me very well, suggested that I needed to be intellectually stimulated. He sensed my restlessness and encouraged me to return to school, promising me that he would take over some of my duties around the house. I was delighted, excited and scared. What would I do once I returned to school?

I had graduated from college with a major in English literature before I was married. I tried my hand in a few English courses when I began graduate study, but found that I was not as interested in this discipline as I had been when younger. Out of some sense of disappointment and frustration, I sat down to do some serious soul-searching. What did I want, what would I do best, and how could I achieve it?

One constant in my life has always been that other people would come to me with their problems. More specifically, women were always coming to me with their problems. I had some female friends who were in therapy who reported having some difficulty in getting their male therapists to "understand" their problems. There seemed to be a real need for a further exploration of the female psyche and the problems that are peculiar to it.

I recalled reading a quotation from Freud in a general psychology course in undergraduate school. During those days when I was struggling with the decision of what discipline to commit myself to, it reverberated over and over in my mind:

> That is all I had to say to you about femininity. It is certainly incomplete and fragmentary and does not always sound friendly. But do not for-

> get that I have only been describing women in so far as their nature is determined by their sexual function. It is true that the influence extends very far; but we do not overlook the fact that an individual woman may be a human being in other respects as well. If you want to know more about femininity, enquire from your own experience of life, or turn to the poets, or wait until science can give you deeper and more coherent information.[1]

With all due respect to Freud as the founder of modern psychoanalysis, and with the acknowledgment that I have plucked this passage out of context, I consider this remark very limited. The unknowing attitude that Freud demonstrates regarding the "dark continent" (Freud's phrase, used elsewhere, referring to psychological knowledge concerning femininity) inspired me to work toward the illumination of just what that "continent" might be. I decided to become a therapist and to specialize in female psychology.

I picked up courses in psychology which would allow me to apply for graduate school. I had to go back to school with students who were much younger than myself. This, surprisingly enough, revitalized rather than depressed me. I was stimulated by their curiosity, their youth, their idealism. If I had been restless in my existence as a housewife, I was now thriving and alive in my role as a student, pursuing a subject that I loved. All of the brain cells that had been dormant were now reawakening. I knew I had made the right decision.

When I did enter graduate school it became obvious that, in the majority of courses, there was a decided emphasis on male, rather than female, psychology. This, I supposed, was appropriate because most psychological studies use male rather than female subjects for experimentation. I had yet to discover the many implications that result from the male domination of this field.

The course of my own future work unraveled before me one day when I came upon a scientific study conducted by two men, John Paul Brady and Eugene E. Levitt, which determined what males found to be most sexually stimulating.[2] The male subjects were asked to look at photographs representing various sexual activities and to rate them in order of preference.

Reasonable enough, I thought, as I naively and somewhat eagerly turned the pages to discover what females found to be sexually stimulating. What I found in the next few pages was a description of "coefficients," "correlations," "variables," and somewhat confusing statistical patterns. There were no references to similar data on female sexual preferences. As this material was not included, I (again naively) assumed that there must be some sort of oversight or mistake. I went to my professor and asked if he could please direct me to the material that explored female sexual preferences. He looked at me as if he had no idea what I was talking about and also as if I had finally confirmed to him the indelible quality of my stupidity. He did, however, suggest that I look into *Psychological Abstracts,* a bibliographic reference tool that lists every psychological experiment that has ever been conducted in the United States and abroad. I dutifully spent the next two years searching.

What those painful two years taught me is that very little research had been done on the issues of female sexual responses and preferences. They also taught me that most of the few studies that had been attempted were highly informed and influenced by the findings of Alfred Kinsey's *Sexual Behavior in the Human Female,*[3] a book based on the research study conducted in 1953.

This is not to say that females have been completely ignored by the scientific discipline of psychology. Many studies address themselves to the behavior and attitudes of women in their social roles—wives, mothers, career women, especially in more recent years when female psychologists have been involved in active research. And, in the last decade, the works of Masters and Johnson, Helen Singer Kaplan, Lonnie Garfield Barbach, and others have been instrumental in breaking new ground in articulating techniques of sexual functioning for women.[4]

What surprised me when I was first beginning to look into specific research on how women felt about sexual responses and activities was the imbalance between the numbers of studies that focused on how men felt and thought about sex and the relative absence of studies that focused on how women felt and thought about it.

I came to feel so frustrated that I began to imagine that if you took all the research that had been done on the topic of sexuality in males and put it in a pile on the floor, the pile would reach to the ceiling. If you took all the research done on the topic of sexuality in females, you could fit it quite nicely into an 8½ x 11 manila envelope. Conversely, I began to think I understood what men might feel when they looked at all the numbers and variety of books and studies that have addressed themselves to the topic of "mothering," compared to the relatively few devoted to the subject of "fathering." Both sexes, in their own ways, have been victims of, if not complete neglect, certainly an imbalance of interest and attention.

When I realized how little focus had been placed on sexuality in females, I was rather staggered. What amazed me was that male researchers did not seem to be interested in what females preferred sexually. Males dominate the field of psychological research. One would imagine that it would be to their own best interest and advantage to study this area of female sexuality in order to be one step ahead of the game, at least in their personal lives. Apparently not, for the emphasis is most definitely on what males think, feel, and prefer about sex.

When I looked at this situation somewhat more objectively, I assumed that one logical reason why female sexuality had been neglected by male researchers might be that they were uncomfortable with the intimate details involved. They seemed more comfortable maintaining the mystery of femininity and keeping the continent "dark."

I knew then just what my course of study would be: I would do my research on female sexuality, specifically female sexual preferences. That research is the basis for the present book. In my study, the results of which are presented in chapters 4, 5 and 6, I extended my experiment to include both male and female subjects and also to cover the predictions of sexual preference for the same and the opposite sex.

I did this initially because I wanted my research to be as comprehensive and relevant as possible so that it could be of use to professionals—sex therapists, gynecologists, psychiatrists, and psychologists. I soon realized that the work I was doing was revealing information that is important to everyone—professionals, lay people, any man or woman involved with a member of the opposite sex.

Now that I am a therapist in private practice, dealing almost exclusively with women, I see more than ever the need for this and further research into the topic of sexuality. You will see that throughout the book I refer from time to time to my clinical experiences to support some of the discoveries that have emerged from my own research as well as to point out some areas that still require elucidation.

I once met a very old and very wise Greek woman. When she sensed trouble brewing among members of her family, she would utter a phrase in her native tongue. Translated, it meant, "I ring a bell of warning." In writing this book, I ring a bell of warning to alert the men and women who are reading it to the problem at hand.

It is time we took steps to determine, from the overwhelming variety of popular descriptions and definitions of sex, what is actually occurring in the areas of female and male sexuality. Men and women are now left to formulate their own notions of what the opposite sex wants and prefers. We must stop working from the speculative premises of assumption, conjecture, and myth and begin to search for a solid ground of reality.

I hope this book will help by addressing itself to some of the reasons for the difficulties in communication between the sexes and that it will provide some information about the specific sexual preferences of females and males as garnered through a scientifically controlled experiment. I also hope that, from this information, we can look forward to fresher attitudes as well as new forms of behavior and expression between sexual partners.

WHY is it difficult for adults to convey to each other their truest sexual preferences? There are, of course, a number of rather complicated emotional and psychological reasons. One important ingredient is the different kinds of training and conditioning we experience as young males and females.

Children, like adults, are human animals, and they begin their lives with their own temperament and personality. It used to be assumed that the child began life with an unmarked psyche, a *tabula rasa,* or clean slate, that awaited the impressions of the parent. In more recent years, researchers have discovered that the process of cognitive development in children is much more complicated than this earlier view of dominant external influence and control.

In *Beyond Sugar & Spice,* Caryl Rivers, Rosalind Barnett, and Grace Baruch provide ample, well-documented examples of studies that suggest that "the parenting process [is] a two-way street, in which the characteristics of the child have a profound impact on the actions of the parents."[1] Other studies reveal that parents are often quite unaware of the methods they use to socialize their children, and that there are some very significant developmental implications attached to those areas in which parents treat boys and girls very differently.[2]

Let us return to the idea that children are human animals. As humans, they have the equipment of a backlog of memory, experience, and capacity to learn and grow. They are prepared to use their minds to put information given to them into meaningful patterns. As animals, they possess instincts that exist in both their pre- and postnatal experiences.[3] As children, then, we exist with animal instincts intact and with minds that develop in interaction with the adult world that guides us in the use and control of our feelings.

It is from adults that children learn what they should or should not do, what is right, what is wrong, and how to tell the difference. The adults provide children with an information system that determines how they think and how they act. We can imagine this information in a child's mind affecting both his attitudes and his behavior.

Now let's look at some of the sources of specific sexual attitudes and behavior available to children. We know that in some areas it is going to differ for boys and girls. First, what kind of voice and what types of sounds run through the mind of a girl child? From the time she is very small, a female receives strong messages that her sexuality is, in general, not such a good thing.

A little girl raised in any contemporary Westernized culture soon learns that her genital area is a "no-no," a place that is not to be explored or discussed. The result is that many young women are actually ignorant about the anatomical structure of their own bodies. One young woman came to my office with the problem of a negative body image. She reported her dismay when the clitoral-vaginal controversy was raised. "I couldn't believe people were discussing this as a problem; I didn't even know I *had* one. I knew I had a vagina. I did not know I had a clitoris."

Of course there is some theoretical foundation for a woman's denial of her clitoral area. Freud was the first to theorize about what he termed "the discovery of the inferiority of the clitoris," which he felt was the most important effect of female penis envy.[4] Freud held that stimulation of the clitoris was a masculine, not a feminine, activity and that, in order to fully develop as a female, a woman had to eliminate her own clitoral sexuality. In other words, once a woman recognizes her clitoris as a sexual organ, she must label it as masculine and quickly abandon it if she is to get on with her development as a female.

This predominantly masculine approach to the subject of female sexuality, specifically of the clitoris, was upheld by followers of Freud and other prominent psychologists and eventually filtered down into popular consciousness. Fortunately, this view of the clitoris as an immature and masculine function of femininity has since been refuted, and, according to the data provided by *The Hite Report,* women are beginning to practice and enjoy clitoral stimulation quite regularly.[5] This is occurring, apparently, even in spite of their backgrounds. One of Hite's subjects reported that her enlightened and sexually liberated mother "Told me about every part of my body except my clitoris."[6]

Feminine denial of the clitoris is only one part of a general depreciation and deprecation of the female genitalia. One of the first lessons a female learns in toilet training is to use toilet tissue each time she urinates. She is usually taught that she should never touch herself in that area while urinating and that, following any contact with her genitals, she must wash her hands.

It is not surprising that a little girl who has been instructed to wash her hands even when the only thing she has touched is toilet tissue begins to get the idea that her genitals much be dirty and unpleasant. She starts to think of her genital area as a place which should be avoided and which must be extremely unattractive to other people.

On the other hand, as part of her process of growth, a young female feels the need to explore her body. While nature and instinct prod her to examine her genitals, mother and/or grandmother do not. Young females get little support for their need to find out who and what they are physically, unless, of course, they are blessed with extremely enlightened parents. The typical adult reaction to a little girl's interest in her genitals is, "That's not a nice thing to do," "Good girls don't do that," and "That's naughty," (Forthcoming data will reveal some surprising information about how adult women respond to oral sex.)

Every time a little girl meets with disapproval from influential adults, the negative voice about her own sexuality is confirmed and strengthened. She learns to discourage or ignore the natural process of sexuality developing within her. She also learns to defend herself against any subsequent sexual feeling. In other words, the voice from her childhood continues and grows through adolescence and even into mature adulthood. Sexual guilt in a female begins when she is a little girl; it does not end when she becomes a grown woman. Many women report that during sexual activity they can still hear the disapproving voice, the voice that tells them they are being dirty, bad, and naughty, even when they are within a sanctioned marriage bed.

Dr. Leah Schaefer conducted and wrote one of the first serious studies of the subjective experience of female sexuality: *Women and Sex.* She found that most women associated their initial experience of intercourse with feelings of confusion, guilt, and irrationality. Many of the married women in the study reported that they experienced no pleasure whatsoever when they first had sex with their new husbands. One woman expressed it this way:

> "As I recall now, the intercourse itself was not only painful but also an unpleasant experience. I only did it because this was what he wanted, and I was sort of giving in. I don't remember it

as being enjoyable at all. . . . I felt disgusted and ashamed."[7]

The early negative feelings towards their genitals that many women learn as girls, as Dr. Schaefer's findings confirm, do not simply vanish along with the advent of acne and other painful problems of adolescence. They remain within the maturing female and emerge each time she experiences a sexual feeling or engages in a sexual activity. Adults who discourage children from bodily exploration and from indulgence in sexual curiosity should know that they are interfering in a way that will have ramifications far into the future.

One of the reasons that adults discourage such physical investigation is that they fear it will lead to masturbation, a cultural taboo for most middle-class American families. When I was in high school, one of my friends revealed to me that she had once been caught in the act of masturbating with a Coke bottle by her mother and her grandmother. Apparently, the bottle had become stuck in her vagina.

This situation might have been seen as either laughable or treated as an accident with some potential for danger. In this household it was not. Her mother's response to the scene was disgust, her grandmother's that of undisguised horror. My friend said that for many months afterward she felt shame, humiliation, self-disgust, and, above all, out-and-out guilt. When I asked her if she continued to masturbate after this incident, she said yes. The lesson for parents is that admonitions and punishments that are doled out over a child's practice of masturbation do not prevent the child from masturbating. They merely add an associative guilt to the experience.

My friend was rare in that she dared to discuss such a matter with another female. I think it is safe to say that the majority of adolescent females in this country do masturbate. In researching for his book, *Teenage Sexuality,* Aaron Hass asked a sampling of fifteen- to eighteen-year-old boys and girls how frequently they masturbated.[8] The responses ranged from more than once a day to less than once a month, but not a single subject replied that he or she had never masturbated. Hass also found that the negative parental messages that teenagers receive cause them considerable upset and distress. Most adolescents who masturbate—and the majority of them do—express feelings of guilt, shame, dirt, stupidity, embarrassment, or abnormality.[9]

The guilt that surrounds the practice of masturbation is compounded for females because of the negative associations they have been taught to attach to their genitals. Not only are they doing something "bad," they are invading forbidden territory. This causes a female adolescent, even if she masturbates only infrequently, considerable discomfort with her self-image.

Of course, it is not only girls who become victims of negative feelings about masturbation. Boys are often warned that they will develop warts, hair on the palm, severe acne, and other imagined (for they are not real) disasters if they dare to indulge in masturbation. Even in this decade, where masturbation is being more frequently researched and openly discussed, young and developing males still suffer remnants of guilt for engaging in this solitary sex act. The difference with males is that they talk to each other about sexual activities, including masturbation, and that males generally have positive and appreciative attitudes about their penises. As a result, males do not feel as lonely or guilty as do females. They can reassure themselves that what they do is typical and "all right."

Females are not so fortunate. Their sexual response is much more limited by learning and cultural dictates, and females hesitate to discuss their sexual activities with each other. Their experiences tend to be isolated and private. Many of my patients express, for example, intense disapproval of activities like masturbation and premarital sex—even those who admit to fairly liberal and permissive sexual attitudes and behavior.

One patient told me that as a child she masturbated constantly, even though she knew she would be punished if found out. She also told me that she was never able to discuss this practice with anyone except her husband. Apparently, when she revealed to him that she enjoyed masturbation, he responded very positively, much to her surprise. I think this is an important lesson as to why most women do not talk to others about masturbation: masturbation implies a personal admission of sexual desire and feeling.

Another patient confided in her best friend when she was in adolescence. She told her that she had let her boyfriend feel her breasts and manipulate her nipples and then began, with considerable enthusiasm, to tell her friend how sexually excited she became and how she felt a swelling sensation in her vagina.

The friend was horrified and, although my patient could sense this, there was no turning back in terms of telling her story. Eventually, the friend stopped calling and finally dropped her. Unfortunately, my patient took a risk in communicating sexual feeling to a friend, and she lost.

I believe that the girl friend made what she believed to be an appropriate "nice girl" response. Based on her previous learning experiences, everything my patient was telling her was "not nice." The upshot was, however, that she judged and condemned her friend for having natural sexual feelings. Boys would not have handled the situation in this way. A boy probably would have requested further details and, rather than judging his friend harshly, would have applauded and praised him for "scoring."

We have seen how the small girl's head gets filled with information about what is bad about sexual activities. By adolescence, the young woman knows that she should not have contact with her genitals, that her female parts are unpleasant and unclean, that masturbation is unnatural and evil, and that to engage in either fondling herself or actual masturbation is to pay the enormous price of guilt.

With all this running through her mind, she seems to get final confirmation of the negative associations she has been taught from her very own body when she begins to menstruate. As a young woman begins the menstrual cycle, she perceives that the process of menstruation is associated with an array of emotional and physical infirmities. A 1978 study of pre- and postmenarcheal (menstrual) girls reports that "a girl enters menarche with a clear set of expectations, many of which are quite negative; and most of her peers, both male and female, hold similar expectations. Her experience of menstruation is, therefore, primed to be a self-fulfilling prophecy."[10]

My work with female patients confirms the negative feelings that surround a female's initiation into menstruation. One woman described to me the elaborate arrangements her mother made to keep the fact of the daughter's menstruation secret from the father. When I asked if she had any clue as to her mother's reasons, she said: "My mother told me that if my father ever found out he would get sick and angry." Frequently women tell me that they fear that their husbands or lovers are repelled by the menstrual blood.

It is generally accepted that the roots of distaste

and anxiety over menstruation can be traced to cultural taboos, often religiously generated. The Bible outlines rules for "ceremonial uncleanliness" in Leviticus 15:19–30. Here is what the holy scripture recommends about dealing with a menstruating woman:

> When a woman has a discharge of blood which is her regular discharge from her body, she shall be in her impurity for seven days; and whoever touches her shall be unclean until the evening./ And everything upon which she lies during her impurity shall be unclean; everything also upon which she sits shall be unclean./And whoever touches her bed shall wash his clothes; and bathe himself in water, and be unclean until evening./ And whoever touches anything upon which she sits shall wash his clothes, and bathe himself in water, and be unclean until evening;/whether it is the bed or anything upon which she sits, when he touches it he shall be unclean until the evening./And if any man lies with her, and her impurity is on him, he shall be unclean seven days; and every bed on which he lies shall be unclean.
>
> If a woman has a discharge of blood for many days, not at the time of her impurity, or if she has a discharge beyond the time of her impurity, all the days of the discharge she shall continue in uncleanliness; as in the days of her impurity, she shall be unclean. . . ./But if she is cleansed of her discharge, she shall count for herself seven days, and after that she shall be clean./ And on the eighth day she shall take two turtledoves or two young pigeons, and bring them to the priest, to the door of the tent meeting./And the priest shall offer one for a sin offering and

> the other for a burnt offering; and the priest shall make atonement for her before the LORD for her unclean discharge.

It is truly unfortunate that this attitude toward women, perpetrated by men with limited understanding of the actual function of menstruation, is still in force today. Contemporary men are, of course, far more enlightened about the process. If you were to ask a male gynecologist, for example, if he considers menstruation an "unclean time," he would probably laugh and ask you to join the twentieth century with the rest of us. However, my practice provides ample proof that the history of beliefs and attitudes that have surrounded menstruation still affects the behavior and attitudes of both men and women today.

In fact, a very attractive patient of mine tells me that her husband announced to her on the eve of their wedding that he would never, under any circumstances, make love while she, as he put it, "had the curse." Another patient, also quite attractive and with no apparent physical cause to feel undesirable, claims that her husband pleads with her to have sex during her period, telling her that she's sexy, beautiful, and womanly when she is menstruating. She, however, is completely unable to allow sexual intimacy during this time because she feels "unsexy, ugly, horrid" when she menstruates.

The negative feelings that a woman has over her own process of menstruation are aggravated by advertisements in the media that heartily celebrate such phenomenon as "feminine hygiene" and condemn "feminine odor." These are some of the specters women have had to confront in their physical and emotional development.

The feminine deodorant sprays and other similar products are marketed through magazine and television ads in ways that suggest that the use of this product should not be limited to the time of the menstrual period. This type of advertising confirms for women the lessons that they learn very early: their very being necessitates the use of special devices to insure themselves against offending everyone around them.

I was once discussing this problem with one of my patients who happens to be an advertising executive. She, like most women, has experienced the embarrassment and pain of imaginary feminine odor and she, unlike other women, has gone beyond these feelings to place the issue in a clear and healthy perspective. After discussing with me the somewhat ridiculous dimension of marketing feminine deodorant sprays, she wrote up the following sketch for a television advertisement:

> Four men and one woman are riding in an elevator. The woman, nervous enough about being eyed by four male strangers, suddenly begins to squirm uncomfortably and then nearly dies of embarrassment as a booming voice that comes from nowhere echoes resoundingly: "DO YOU HAVE F.O.?" (feminine odor). The men, of course, are equally uncomfortable and express this by staring at the floor. They stoically resist holding their noses. When they all reach the top floor, three of the men keel over from the stench, and the fourth, bravely enduring, looks directly at the woman, pulls from his pocket a sample of the current most popular feminine spray, and says: "Put your money where your ———is."

In promoting feminine hygiene products, advertisers are capitalizing on the negative feelings a woman has about her body *and* on yet another myth that has been placed in the mind of the developing female: "You exist to please a male." The philosopher Descartes found the meaning of life in his mental processes, *Cogito ergo sum,* or "I think, therefore I exist." Women are taught that their meaning in life lies in their ability to please and capture the attention of men: "I please, therefore I exist."

Elizabeth Janeway has presented an excellent argument for the economic and social reasons behind a woman's need to please a man in her book *Man's World, Woman's Place,*[11] and there is no reason to repeat that argument here. What I am discussing is the psychological negation a woman feels if she sees herself solely in the role of pleasing men. This demand causes a woman to feel that her own identity is insignificant, and that she should remain passive and compliant in her emotional and sexual relations with men.

This internalization of cultural expectation usually means that a female hesitates to express her own sexual desires, rarely initiates sexual activity with a male partner, assumes that he knows better than she what will feel good (even to her own body), and, all too frequently from what I hear from my female patients, finds herself faking orgasms when she is, in fact, left in a state of sexual suspension and frustration.

When a woman thinks and behaves in this way, it confirms men's suspicions that women really are and prefer to be passive and compliant. The vicious cycle continues: Women behave in ways that support men's learned attitudes about them and thus men continue to treat women as completely different from themselves, almost as if they were a different species. Why, given his experience with passive and compliant women, would a man conceive of a woman's having sexual desires and fantasies that are similar to his own? How, believing them to be satisfied with the most traditional and conventional forms of sexual activity, would he feel comfortable in suggesting to his partner that they engage in any activity that might be construed as "kinky sex"?

There is small doubt that the new thinking about relations between the sexes will help to make this kind of feminine self-denial and the resultant misunderstandings between men and women less common. Programs such as assertiveness training and personal growth workshops are current attempts to get women thinking in new and self-directed ways. Hopefully, we will also begin to initiate programs for men that would enable them to identify and understand the social and cultural conditioning that directs them to feel and to act as they do. For both sexes, however, it will take considerable time to unlearn the patterns of attitudes and behavior that have been encouraged for years and years.

Another inhibiting factor in the developing sexuality of young females is the social injunction that forbids them to permit young males to "have their way." Females are expected to adopt a "gatekeeper" approach in their relationships with sexually interested males. Just at the time when a woman begins to feel strong sexual impulses and promptings, she is taught that in the dating game she must play the role of a cool creature and deny all sexual feeling. She is the one who is expected to set the limits.

Even in today's supposedly liberated sexual climate, it is the female who is expected to say no. Recent research maintains that a woman still is seen as ultimately responsible for deciding whether or not intercourse will occur and that male pressure often makes it difficult for her to uphold the socially sanctioned standards.[12] Males are expected to want to engage in heavy petting and intercourse; females are expected to control both their own and the male's desire toward such an end. This means that most female adolescents experience considerable conflict and stress over sexuality. One adult woman expressed it to me this way:

> I remember feeling both pleased and guilty about attracting boys. If they liked me, I felt that I was "ok," but I never really knew how to handle their attention. I didn't know what was expected of me. Once a boy showed interest in me and we started to date, I was faced with whether or not to give in to his sexual desires or to be called a "tease." When he had an erection or got horny, I felt it was my fault, and yet I also felt responsible for keeping things under control. It seemed all right for boys to have desires and to perform sex, but not all right for girls. I was taught that a girl was not supposed to have sexual feelings, that she should always be cool and controlled. Guys married "nice" girls; they just fooled around with "bad" ones.

If we assume (and I do) that women possess sex drives as men do, we must acknowledge that in order to successfully perform this gatekeeper function, young women are forced to restrict and deny their responses to their own bodies, their partner's bodies and to most forms of erotic stimulation. This forced conditioning does not simply dissolve once a woman decides to marry or to take a lover. It hangs on and throws her into a considerable amount of confusion and anxiety.

One of my patients told me that soon after her marriage she began to deeply regret not having had premarital sex with her husband. She felt that she had very little to offer her husband because she had been brought up with very restrictive and rigid attitudes about sexuality. "My mother always told me that sex was bad unless you loved the man and were married to him. Well I'm married and I love my husband, but sex is still bad."

Another married patient told me of a trick she played with herself. After having sex with her lover, she always pretended that it was for the first time. She had such deep feelings of guilt about having sex outside of marriage that she tried to relieve them by "transforming" herself back into a virgin, thinking that she was "purer" and more desirable to the man.

There used to be a strong cultural impetus to remain virginal until marriage. Women who were raised with this expectation in mind cannot be expected to simply abandon all of their previous training and begin to live a life of sexual enjoyment and fulfillment as an adult wife and/or lover.

Today many young women feel the opposite kind of pressure: they feel that they *should* lose their virginity before marriage, and that perhaps there is something wrong with them if they don't. It is very important to recognize that these young women are still experiencing highly contradictory and conflicting feelings about their sexual behavior.

In a comprehensive study of American adolescent behavior in the 1950s, Elizabeth Douvan and Joseph Adelson discovered striking differences in the ways in which boys and girls experienced the process of separating from their parents:

> To sum up, we may say that the line of moral development in girls moves from a rather passive, childlike acceptance of parental authority to an identification with the point of view of authority. As far as we can tell from our evidence, the transition is affected without any intervening phase in which the girl defiantly asserts her own values and controls before moving closer to her parents.[13]

There is still little question that girls more strictly adhere to the parental imperative than do boys, and this causes them more serious difficulties when they are encouraged by their peers to engage in sexual activity. Girls, for example, tend to feel that premarital sex should be predicated on the fact that the partners are in love.

When asked about how they felt about losing their virginity, a large number of the girls in Hass's study reported negative feelings:

> "I was disappointed because I was used by a boy who had no feelings for me at all."
>
> "I felt guilty because I should have waited for the right person to come along."
>
> "I always thought I'd lose my virginity to someone I loved. I realized later I didn't love him and it was kind of a let-down."[14]

My point here is that even though more and more girls are losing their virginity before marriage, they still carry feelings of guilt and conflict over the "promiscuous" relationships they have during developmental years. The guilt that a woman builds up about sex in her childhood and adolescence usually remains with her through mature adulthood. As Catherine Chilman points out in *Adolescent Sexuality in a Changing American Society,* research indicates that premarital sex is often associated for females with feelings of low self-esteem and passive-dependent behavior.[15] It is partially for these reasons that women have such difficulty in admitting and expressing what is sexually pleasurable and preferable to them. The design of my study, however, forced women to seriously examine and express the positive side of their preferences.

Anthropologist Margaret Mead has discussed some other reasons why women feel ambivalent about their own needs and desires in her book *Male and Female.*[16] One reason is that, in the face of social arrangements and cultural prohibitions, a female is never really trained in how to handle the results of her conditioning and acculturation. She is taught to *be* rather than *do*:

> Stage after stage in women's life histories thus stand, irrevocable, indisputable, accomplished. This gives a natural basis for the little girl's emphasis on being rather than doing. The little boy learns that he must act like a boy, and prove it over and over again, while the little girl learns that she is a girl, and all she has to do is refrain from acting like a boy.[17]

American culture has arranged sex roles in such a way that a man is expected to act and conquer, and a woman is expected to respond to him, either by "holding out" before marriage or "giving in" after. This rather strange but painfully familiar set of circumstances leaves a female little room for independent choice and action.

A woman feels that she must please the man, either by remaining virginal or by fulfilling his sexual needs. If she chooses the latter, his preferences take precedence over hers, and her own desires and needs are, in her own mind, regarded as bad, wrong, abnormal and/or irrelevant. Under these conditions, it is small surprise that a woman would not be open and expressive about her own sexual pleasures.

In a speaking engagement where I was discussing this phenomenon of female suppression and silence, a woman of about forty-five volunteered the information that earlier in her marriage her husband had purchased a book about sex. In her secretive readings of this book, the woman found herself becoming aroused and increasingly interested in having sexual relations with her husband.

She felt incapable of expressing this excitement to him, however. When asked why, she replied that she had felt embarrassment and shame about her feelings. "I was convinced," she said, "that he would think I was vulgar." When she found this book, this woman had been having sex with her husband for twenty-three years, and she still could not feel comfortable expressing active interest in new forms of sexual activity. This is an all-too-familiar situation, where both partners lose!

Evidently the man in this relationship was interested in improving and expanding the sexual relationship with his wife or he wouldn't have bought the book. He apparently felt, however, that he could not raise the topic of sex with her, and instead left the book around for her to find on her own. As it turned out, his wife was highly responsive to the idea. The book, if acknowledged and accepted by both, could have provided this couple with a tool of communication that could have opened new doors between them. The husband's hesitations and the wife's feelings of guilt and shame over experiencing arousal and sexual drive were, in this case, the controlling inhibitive factors.

These negative feelings about sexuality form one of the biggest barriers in the communication process between men and women. Quite frequently, for example, in order to fulfill her role of pleasing a man, a woman will deny her own needs and lie about achieving an orgasm. The result is that he is deluded and she is frustrated. They can then get into a habit, as we sketched in the introduction, of his thinking that she is satisfied with the activities he performs and her thinking that she cannot express the truth for fear of hurting his feelings.

This is most definitely a no-win situation, and it can and does continue for years, indeed for the life spans of some marriages. One woman who was interviewed on the subject of sexual expression stated: "It was thirty years before I worked up the courage to tell my husband what I liked [sexually], thirty wasted years!" "I suffered unbearable frustration," another woman said, "because I could not bring myself to tell my husband what he was doing wrong. By the time I worked up the courage, he had lost most of his interest in sex."[18]

Isn't it time we began to learn from these situations? Can't we look at these sufferings and begin to see how they can be eliminated by growth and change? I think we can. We can, for example, begin raising our daughters so that they can have healthy and positive feelings about their bodies and their sexuality. Also, we can suggest to those women who do have problems in sexual assertion that they experiment with new and alternative forms of expression and behavior. Both of these issues will be discussed in later chapters. For now, let's look at some of the difficulties men have in communicating their sexual preferences to women.

We have listened to some of the sounds of the voice that speaks to women; what are some of the sounds heard by men? What patterns of training and conditioning occur in the development of male sexuality that directly influence a male's inability to communicate sexually?

In a recent book addressing male sexuality, authors Anthony Pietropinto and Jacqueline Simenauer report their findings in a study they conducted to determine how men view women, what men look for and don't look for in women, and what men like to do sexually with women. The book *Beyond the Male Myth*[19] indicates that male attitudes and behavioral patterns are in transition and some of the study's findings confirm my own.

While the authors admonish contemporary writers who fail "to perceive the change that has taken place in men over the past few years," and who expect males "to persist in the traditions that governed them more than a decade ago,"[20] they themselves point to some fairly persistent patterns that cause men difficulties in sexual attitude and behavior.

If, for example, a man cannot achieve an erection when he is sexually involved with a woman, his entire sexual identity is threatened.

> While experts point out that he can still receive and give sexual satisfaction in other ways, we have found . . . that men regard intercourse as their prime source of feeling manly, and the prospect of a sexual encounter without an erection would be as distressing as entering a golf tournament without a club.[21]

It is culturally determined that a man's role is to dominate and control the sexual situation and, therefore, his ability to perform is critical. Some of the myths surrounding male domination and control will take an interesting turn as my study results are revealed.

The demand to perform and satisfy his female partner can be very distressing to a male. Since he is expected to bring a woman to the heights of ecstasy, failure in sexual performance can be devastating to a male ego. If he experiences premature ejaculation and cannot bring his partner to orgasm, a man ofen feels guilt and a deep sense of personal failure.[22]

The training that a male receives early in childhood often limits his ability to be open and expressive in emotional and sexual relationships. Males in the American culture are not encouraged to develop intimate, physically and emotionally close relationships. They are encouraged to be independent. Douvan and Adelson discuss this rather dramatic difference between the developing sexes:

> For the boy . . . the integrated capacity for erotic ties and the solution of the identity challenge demand separation and autonomy. What the girl achieves through intimate connection with others, the boy must manage by disconnecting, by separating himself and asserting his right to be distinct.[23]

Boys, then, are taught to manage their independence by standing on their own two feet and declining any indulgence in close intimacy with others. This includes physical intimacy, and boys experience much less opportunity for touching and for bodily contact with others than do girls.

This, along with other developmental issues that separate the sexes in adolescence, causes awkward and strained relations between males and females. As the need to touch and be touched is strongly instinctual for both sexes, boys who experience deprivation of this need in early developmental years often feel a compulsion to "make up" for the loss in their adolescent years.

Just at a time when a girl is being taught to control her sexual feelings, to suppress erotic impulses, and simulate a lack of interest in sex, the boy she is dating is feeling the need to "catch up" on all the touching, fondling, and caressing that he missed earlier. This situation does not encourage a happy and communicative combination. At times young women report being overwhelmed by the male need for intense physical contact.

One of the most unfortunate consequences of this incompatibility is that in order to find release for the physical tension and in order to learn about sexual behavior with women, adolescent males usually have to turn to prostitutes or "tramps" for their initial sexual experiences. These encounters are most often unsatisfactory and the young male begins to associate sexual expression and release with negative images of women.

If he chooses to go to a prostitute, he is most likely hurried through the experience. It is to the prostitute's advantage to get him to achieve orgasm as quickly as possible because it is at this point that her job is finished and she gets paid. The quicker he comes, the more tricks she turns, the more money she makes.

If he decides to take out the local tramp, the girl that everyone knows "puts out," he usually finds himself frantically having intercourse in the back seat of a car. In this situation, the young man fears being caught or found out. He never knows when authority may appear in the form of a policeman with a flashlight and so, as in the situation with the prostitute, he tries to get through the sexual encounter as quickly as possible.

In both situations, he attempts to achieve climax without foreplay and without learning anything about a woman's body or what activities most stimulate her. These initial experiences of sex leave a male in conflict between his intense need for sexual release and his feelings of guilt, disgust, emotional frustration, and ignorance. He usually has to mask these feelings in locker-room conversations where he is asked to fulfill the image of the virile male who is the wonder and delight of all females.

Another conflict that a developing adolescent male experiences in this culture is often described as the "madonna-whore" complex. Men are taught in their relationships with their mothers and sisters that a woman is to be respected and adored, to be put on a pedestal and kept from all things unpleasant. Such women, of course, have no sexual needs of their own.

When a young man becomes aware of his sexual feelings toward women, his respect and considerations for those women closest to him demand that he turn toward other types of women for sexual release and expression. Consciously he is unable to think of women he admires as sexual objects. He has to create a whole other category of females who would appropriately absorb his feelings of desire and lust.

The adolescent male makes a distinction in his mind between those women who are available for his sexual need (whores) and those women who must be placed above it (madonnas). The real emotional problem results when he finds a woman with whom he wants sex, but toward whom he also wants to be able to maintain respect. In trying to bridge the gap between those women he can sleep with and those he cannot, he becomes extremely solicitous and considerate to his chosen partner. This makes it very difficult for him to communicate his real sexual preferences to her. He feels that she should be kept away from the full force of his lust, and so he develops with her "conventional" and "acceptable" forms of sexual behavior.

Part of this conflict stems from the training a male gets from his father about the proper relationship a son has with his mother. How many times have we heard fathers say, "Never talk that way to your mother" or, "I don't ever want to hear you use a word like that in front of your mother"? Women, especially women he loves, appear to the young boy as creatures who must remain unstained and unsullied by male concerns, especially male sexuality.

When a male then chooses a female as a partner whose destiny it is to become the mother of his children, he feels the responsibility to maintain the sense of her "purity." While he has no trouble in performing intercourse for reproduction, he may have difficulty in asking her to participate in his more unconventional sexual preferences. This reticence severely limits his ability to determine or discuss sexual preferences.

There is another deeper and more psychologically complicated reason why men feel that they must separate females from their developing sexuality, and this is the necessary and painful process of the male detachment and separation from the mother.

Put very simply, the male and female infant both begin life with a total identification with the mother. She is the one who tends to all their needs, provides nourishment, learning, and support. As the child develops, however, there is an important sex differentiation. While girls will experience feelings of resentment and competition in relation to the mother, they never completely isolate or detach themselves from an identification with her. Boys, however, must and do. Boys experience an increasing and continuing need to separate themselves from the mother in order to resolve their Oedipal feelings and also in order to complete the male socialization process, which emphasizes independence, autonomy, and being in control.

There are very important implications here for the difficulties of communication between the sexes. First, in separating his feelings of sexuality from his emotional relationship with his mother, a boy begins to develop an isolated lust, undifferentiated from any specific female. As we know, this is very different from adolescent girls who find the sole justification for having sexual relations with a boy in love and emotional commitment.

Second, in leaving the mother behind, the boy "puts away all things childish," like the tender and loving feelings that were fostered in the emotionally dependent relationship he earlier enjoyed. He tends to view gestures of affection and tenderness as immature and feminine, and may have difficulty recalling or admitting them in a relationship with a female, who has been taught to feel that these signals of intimacy and emotional investment are very important.

Third, there is the whole issue of male control and dominance that accompanies the process of separation from the mother. Robert May, in the book *Sex and Fantasy*, suggests that this issue may transfer or project onto the sexual treatment of women:

> The persistent need to separate from the original matrix and the challenge of learning to master his own potential for energetic activity combine to make the issue of control a central one. Sex may become an extension of this struggle since it offers the illusion of control . . . that sexual conquest provides.[24]

And, last, in separating from the mother, in leaving behind all things feminine and emotionally expressive, males participate in and perpetuate the male-male bond of the Western culture, a bond that often encourages men to regard women as outside of the wider concerns of civilization and possibly as less meaningful to the work of advancement and progress. In so doing, men significantly diminish their capacity and opportunities for healthy and honest communication with women.

We have been discussing the conflicting sounds and themes that males hear in their struggle to become sexually defined and mature. Perhaps one of the most critical sources of instruction for males about their sexuality is the media. Television, movies, magazines, books and billboards emphasize the image of a strong, dominant, virile, and sexually powerful male whose central purpose in life is to seduce, conquer, and subsequently abandon numbers of attractive but intellectually insubstantial females. When the young and relatively inexperienced adolescent boy, struggling with the intense inner feelings we have just reviewed, compares himself to these unrealistic and improbable male media models, he is bound to hear some discords of insecurity, inferiority, and threat.

Probably one of the major reasons that Woody Allen's films are so popular, both in America and abroad, is that they expose the reality behind this *machismo* myth. Men, especially adolescent men, do not always feel wise, confident, dominant, capable, virile, and successful in their sexual relations. Often they feel timid, uncertain, shy, and passive. The myth, however, tells them that they must think and act in certain ways, and most men are extremely hesitant about admitting that they do not always feel they can fulfill the expected and accepted male image.

There are some widely perpetrated assumptions that underline the *macho* philosophy and generate a number of fictions that create the *macho* myth. One of these fictions is that men are masters of sexual expression and natural educators of women in how to be sexually responsive and satisfied. This particular fiction does not hold up in practice. Men have no more assumed claim to sexual wisdom than do women. They should not be expected to possess some secret knowledge about how to make a woman sexually responsive. At times men really appreciate information from a woman about what is most stimulating to her.

The same holds true with the fiction that men are inherently more sexual than women and should therefore initiate and direct the sexual situation. Men do not always want to initiate sexual relations. They sometimes like to be seduced and led, to be passive or receptive. In actuality, there are times when men gratefully accept the role of passivity in sexual relations. They enjoy being kissed, fondled, caressed, and often prefer that the female take the role of aggressor in intercourse, which we will begin to see as the results of the study unfolds.

A final fiction is that men are totally knowledgeable about the female body and female sexuality, and therefore understand how to make a woman most responsive and satisfied. This is simply impossible to believe. Men do not take courses to learn about female anatomy. It would be a rare mother who provided for her son a chart that pointed to and labeled the various erogenous zones of the female body.

Men learn about women from the women with whom they have relationships and from pornography, both hard and soft. We have already discussed the reasons why women are often not completely communicative about what they feel and want sexually, so men have somewhat of a learning disability in their sexual relations with real women. They have a similar problem in their education about women from pornography since, as expert Leslie Farber has written in his article on the differences between the sexes, the pornography industry is dedicated to engaging within men their shared sense of undifferentiated lust.[25] As women more frequently explore their own eroticism through emotional investment and commitment to a single person, pornography provides more of an education about men than it does about women.

At the beginning of this chapter we asked the question: Why is it difficult for adults to convey to each other their truest sexual preferences? From our end-of-the-chapter perspective, we can review some of the reasons for this lack of communication.

First, women are taught to feel that their genitals are dirty and unpleasant. They are not encouraged to explore, define, understand, or accept their genitals as part of their developing womanhood. This means that when they confront the probable experiences of masturbation and the inevitable experiences of menstruation, they suffer feelings of guilt, shame, and irrationality. Very frequently these feelings are transferred onto the experience of sexual intercourse itself, particularly when the young woman has been taught that all of the responsibility for sexual behavior in a dating relationship rests with her.

When a woman does enter into a sexual relationship with a man, she frequently retains feelings of guilt and shame. Added to these is a sense that she should take on the role of pleasing him rather than pursuing her own interests or desires. Often this kind of self-denial becomes habitual in the relationship. A woman can go on for years pretending satisfaction but accepting frustration as a fact of life. A painfully dramatic example is the woman who kept her own needs pent up for thirty years because she could not find the courage to tell her husband that he was not pleasing her. When she did finally bring herself to express this to him, he had lost his interest in sex.

Men do not experience the same kind of early training that women do. They do not harbor feelings of guilt and shame about their "unpleasant" genitals. Quite the contrary, they find their genitals a source of pleasure and pride. Little boys touch their penis every time they urinate. Rather than feel an urgency to wash their hands after urinating as women do, men often wash their hands before urinating so they don't "dirty" their clean penises with their hands.

Also, while females often suffer their sexuality in isolation and silence, males tend to feel freer in sharing ideas and experiences with other males. While men often tend to limit their discussions about sex to locker rooms where no one challenges the validity of their statements, it is clear that men have an unspoken understanding that sex is something they have been granted both permission and responsibility for.

This shared understanding gives to males much

more comfort in their sexual development than females. They feel freer to masturbate, freer to engage in intercourse, freer to experiment with unconventional forms of sexual behavior.

Men are not, however, divorced from some confusions and frustrations that make it difficult for them to express sexual preferences and interests with ease and comfort. Most often feel that they may be unable to perform adequately and that they may be incapable of pleasing and satisfying their partners.

Men are also not encouraged to fondle, kiss, caress and touch others. In turn, they often find it awkward and difficult to develop intimate physical relations with members of either sex. Men also experience the painful separation from the mother as a necessary development with serious and disturbing effects on their relations with females. This discomfort is compounded during the embarrassing period of adolescence when physical and sexual needs intensify. A male may choose to "opt out" and have sex only with prostitutes and tramps rather than risk a sexual encounter with a "nice" girl. These initial encounters are often unsatisfying and tend to associate sexual release with "bad" women in the mind of the adolescent male.

Last, men are often victimized by the false assumptions that surround the myth of the *macho* man. These unrealistic expectations that are placed on a man can do little to foster his honest communications between the sexes, as they encourage a mind set that diminishes women's sexual rights and places an inordinate sexual burden on him.

Now that we have looked at some of the dynamics that underlie male and female development, it is easier to understand why having sex can sometimes become complicated, why people may have trouble expressing their preferences, and even how people may end up facing the same dilemma as poor Marsha and Fred.

In the following pages I will present the conditions

and results of my study of male and female sexual preferences. This reveals that many of the patterns one might expect from social and cultural conditioning of males and females are false. The results of the study are informative, surprising, and enlightening. They show that in the light of actual rather than assumed sexual preference, both males and females express desire for sexual activities that directly contradict the socially defined expectations we have described in this chapter.

2 Methodology of the Study

As I learned in my graduate work and as is still true at the time of this writing, there have been inadequate scientific norms established on female sexual preferences and only poor and limited work on the subject of female sexuality in general. There have been clinical studies, special reports, and fictional writings that address the topic, but none of these presents conclusive scientific evidence that confirms a measurable and valid norm.

One of the few widely known works available to the public on the topic of female sexuality appeared in 1970. Masters and Johnson's *Human Sexual Inadequacy*[1] included some specific information about female sexuality. The book devoted itself primarily to the physiological dimension of sex, specifically to the problems of sexual dysfunction, not sexual normality, in both males and females.

The book was not readily or easily absorbed by lay readers and, therefore, had little impact in enlightening the general public. In fact, a subsequent book, *Masters and Johnson Explained*,[2] was published in the same year. It translated what Masters and Johnson had to say into language that could be understood by the general public.

The importance of these two books for women was that they drew attention to physiological sexual problems that women were actually experiencing. By focusing on phrases like "orgasmic dysfunction" (inability and difficulty to achieve orgasm) and "vaginismus" (involuntary muscular spasms), Masters and Johnson opened up ways for women to begin to be more comfortable in discussing with their gynecologists their problems of sexual dysfunction.

Gynecologists were, unfortunately, ill prepared to respond. The general absence of information on female sexuality has left female-health-care professionals such as gynecologists, obstetricians, and sex therapists sadly and severely handicapped and with few resources for giving women sound advice. In the early years of the 1970s, then, women were still lacking scientific literature and professional guidance to answer questions on their sexual attitudes, preferences, and behaviors.

When we look at the middle and late years of the decade, we can see that women, in compensation for the absence of serious scientific attention paid to their sexuality, and in need of finding forms of expression and communication, turned to nonscientific channels. Women began to publish fiction, personal memoirs, and pop-psychology books that dealt, for the first time, with female sexual interests, needs, and desires from a woman's point of view.

Perhaps the most important and seminal book was Erica Jong's *Fear of Flying,* first published in 1973. Through the creation of her protagonist, Isadora Wing, Jong revealed an intense female sexual sensibility, from a woman's subjective perspective. Isadora complains that women learn about themselves only through men who defensively project their own personal male bias. "I learned what an orgasm was from D. H. Lawrence" and "I learned from Freud that they [women] have deficient superegos . . . because they lack the one thing in the world worth having: a penis."[3]

While Jong was at work formulating the sexual fantasies and adventures of Isadora, Nancy Friday began studying her own and other women's sexual daydreams. In *My Secret Garden,* Friday reported first-person accounts of women's erotic fantasies. Like Jong, Friday confronted the barriers that are built by the male-dominated assumptions about female sexuality. In doing her research, for example, Friday "could not find a doctor or psychiatrist who would intelligently discuss women's sexual fantasies."[4] Knowing that female sexual fantasy existed and finding no printed material on the subject, Friday decided to publish a book devoted to individual women's expressions of their most hidden sexual dreamworlds.

Female reader response to these two books was overwhelming. Finally women were beginning to establish a ground of communication about their sexuality. Jong's courageous attempt to explain herself and her sexual needs, desires, and frustrations *without scientific analysis or male-dominated logic* won her the hearts of millions of American women.

Friday reported that hundreds of women responded in writing, frequently expressing relief and delight that this topic had finally surfaced for exploration and discussion. A common thread in Friday's reader correspondence was, "Thank God you opened up the discussion of women's sexual fantasies. . . . I thought I was the only one who had these ideas. . . . I felt like a pervert, so guilty and alone."[5]

Jong's and Friday's books confirmed that women have long been victims of cultural conditioning and expectation. Once liberated, women feel more fully able to explore a variety of sexual activities, both fantasized and real. Neither author presumed, however, to offer scientific proof in the form of valid measurable data and results of the sexual experience and fantasies they published.

The first woman writer to attempt a scientific approach to female sexuality was Shere Hite, whose *Hite Report* was published first in 1976.[6] This book was the most influential and highly publicized work to come out of the period of feminist exploration into sexuality. Under the heading of the National Organization for Women, Hite mailed out a questionnaire that received responses from three thousand women, ranging in age from fourteen to seventy-eight. These women described in their own words their attitudes, feelings, and experiences about a variety of sexual activities.

Hite's questionnaire was broken down into five parts: orgasm, sexual activities, relationships, and a conclusion appropriately titled "The Ending," which lists generalized questions that could have been placed in the other categories. Women who responded to the questionnaire wrote out answers to fifty-eight questions like "Please describe what an orgasm feels like to you" and "Do you enjoy masturbating?"

I believe that Hite's work is significant in that it established a new frame of reference for female sexuality. Her book was published at a time when women were ready to discuss these topics openly, and the results of her research provided both men and women with the language to do so. Not only were the words, and concepts published in print, they were now ready to be spoken and heard.

The Hite Report generated a great deal of controversy. Many people felt that they could not agree with or accept Hite's findings based on a selective sampling consisting mostly of feminist and educated women. Hite's sampling expressed a bias that placed most of the blame for female frustration and unfulfilled sexuality on men. The response of some women and most men who read the book was suspicion and anger.

In 1977, another, much less celebrated book on female fantasies appeared: *The Fantasy Files* by Dr. Karen Shanor.[7] This book, subtitled "A Study of the Sexual Fantasies of Contemporary Women," presents a broad range of fantasies from women of all ages, classes, and educational levels.

Shanor scrupulously documented the socioeconomic background of her subjects. In eliciting responses through a specific questionnaire, Shanor provides us with a more valid representative sampling of female fantasy than we get, for example, in a book like Nancy Friday's. In fact, Shanor admits that she seriously doubted the validity of one completed questionnaire and consequently left it out of the study.[8]

Perhaps one of the most valuable contributions in the book is the fourth chapter, where Shanor outlines the most popular sexual fantasies of her female subjects. She includes examples and discussions of over thirty fantasies, some of which are sex with an unknown man, sex with a celebrity, seducing a younger man, sex with another woman, group sex, being overpowered or overpowering a man to surrender sexually, and having sex in natural surroundings or forbidden places.

While *The Fantasy Files* is a more academic and scientific work than *The Hite Report*, very few women ever had the opportunity to read it. The book did not reach a wide audience and consequently remains an interesting but ignored attempt to communicate more information on how and what women fantasize sexually.

In the same year that Shanor's work was published, another book that most certainly reached the general public appeared: *The Redbook Report on Female Sexuality*.[9] This study of sexuality of the American female began as a project in *Redbook* magazine. A questionnaire entitled "How Do You Really Feel About Sex?" was published in the October 1974 issue of the magazine. The response was encouraging enough to prompt two sociologists, Carol Tavris and Susan Sadd, to expand the material into a book, which was published three years later.

The basic message of this report was that Americans have nothing to worry about when it comes to sex. The authors brought us the good news that in America wives love their husbands, husbands love their wives, and everybody loves sex. One of the most encouraging findings was that women under forty enjoy and practice oral sex, both cunnilingus and fellatio. If, the *Redbook* authors report, a woman finds oral sex distasteful, she will find other forms of sexual activity distasteful as well and will be inhibited about sex in general.[10]

The problem with the *Redbook* questionnaire was that it was poorly designed. There was simply not a wide enough range of responses to allow for discriminating intelligent choices. When asked how she would evaluate the sexual "aspect" of her marriage, for example, a woman had five choices ranging from "very good" to "very poor." When asked if she had ever performed oral sex on her husband, a woman can respond to choices from "often" to "never."

These limited options must have lead to a variety of interpretations on the part of those who answered the questionnaire. What is "good" for one person is "fair" for another and what is "often" for one woman may be "occasional" for another. The forced-choice questionnaire used in the *Redbook* study does not allow for an accurate sampling of response nor for the theory of relativity. For example, the woman who dislikes performing fellatio may consider her husband's semimonthly request "often," whereas the woman who really enjoys performing fellatio may consider two times a month "occasional."

Even our very hasty review here of some of the recent publications on female sexuality signals a definite need for further exploration and explanation of the topic. On the one hand, we have researchers and clinicians like Masters and Johnson who write about female sexuality in terms of physiological dysfunction on a level that is beyond most readers' comprehension and on the other an entire body of material written by women devoted to the subjective experience of female sexuality. The clinical research is cold, precise and objective and the literature is filled with emotional descriptions of how individual women struggle toward sexual fulfillment.

In between these two alternatives we have works like *The Hite Report* and the *Redbook* study that give us interesting and thought-provoking information about female sexuality but are sketchy or inadequate in terms of accurate scientific data. Through it all, we lack a body of empirical research that can be translated into a comprehensible prose acceptable to both the professional and the lay reader. I hope that my study will help to fill this gap as well as provide all readers with information that will increase their awareness of human sexuality and advance communications between the sexes.

The original research for the study was conducted out of Roosevelt University with the assistance of four professors of psychology. That work has been expanded for the specific purpose of this book.

Certain intrinsic questions must be addressed in any attempt to expand the pool of human knowledge through a report such as mine. These are: What is being determined? Who is being used to determine it? What medium and methodology are employed? How are the results interpreted and used?

For my study, I knew what I wanted to determine. Ever since reading Brady and Levitt's study on male sexual preferences based on nineteen sexual themes, I had been highly motivated to do a similar study on females. I knew of no scientific research on the topic of what females preferred sexually. I had also never heard any of my female friends or patients discuss this topic. When I began to question other professionals, such as my colleagues who were working in sexual therapy, I began to appreciate how limited their knowledge was.

Realizing that there was particularly meager data on the subject of what females preferred sexually and that the available data on what males preferred was limited, in Brady and Levitt's study, to college-age males, I decided to focus my attention on the sexual preferences of adult males and females. Using the original study as a model, I saw my challenge as collecting basic data concerning preferences for various sexual activities. These preferences were to be measured by presenting to subjects—adult males and females—pornographic photographs depicting certain sexual activities, and asking the subjects to report the degree to which they found the photographs to be sexually stimulating.

I acknowledge that it is reasonable to question the meaningfulness of defining sexual preference in this manner, particularly since recent research indicates that fantasy stimulation need not necessarily be directly related to actual sexual behavior.[11] There is also the question of the validity in the relationship between those sexual activities that are fantasized and those that are, in fact, preferred.

For the purpose of my study, I viewed sexual preference as measured by the degree of excitatory response to photographic representations of sexual activities. In other words, along with Brady and Levitt, I am making the assumption that a subject's response to a photograph of a sexual theme would *infer* to some degree his or her preference for this fantasized activity. In no way does this imply that the subject would actually perform this activity. That information would have to be obtained from a study specifically designed to determine this data.

In this study, then, I have measured reactivity to photographic stimuli and inferred from the results a preference for a sexual activity that the subject may never choose to perform. I am taking the position that preference for sexual activities can be measured through a response to fantasized material as represented in the photographs and that what probably cannot be measured through such fantasized material is what a person would actually do.

After clarifying what I wanted to determine, my next step was to find an appropriate sampling, a set of subjects who could help me define this information. When conducting a study of sexuality, there is some necessity for selective sampling in the nature of the persons involved.

I could not, for example, use subjects who were uncooperative or who had moral or religious biases that would invalidate the data. Since I was trying to determine the sexual preferences of an adult majority, I could not choose persons who identified with a minority group that found the medium or the methodology of the study suspect or immoral. I needed *volunteers.*

This need for people who would voluntarily and without pay participate in the study caused me further cautions and concerns. I could not, for example, afford to engage a group of joy riders or people who get their kicks from looking at dirty pictures. Neither could I afford to engage professionals like prostitutes, pornography peddlers, and the like.

At the time I was beginning to design my research project, I was giving lectures to various men's and women's groups in the Chicago area. These included young married couples, single parents, single persons who had never been married, alumnae groups, Kiwanis and Rotary clubs, and a variety of professional groups like university women, women in communications, men and women in publishing and sales.

It occurred to me that from these groups I might obtain a valid sampling. By coming to my talks these people were expressing an interest in my topic, which almost always centered on the differences between male and female sexuality. Also, most of these people were associated with professional, academic, or social organizations, which, I felt, gave them some claim to a legitimate, established civic identity.

Usually at the end of my presentations I would open the floor for questions and comments. I took this opportunity, when questioned about my research, the preparation of materials, the development of research design and other topics, to carefully explain what I intended to determine and what methods I was going to use to determine it. I explained that subjects would be viewing photographs depicting sexual activities and that anyone who would have difficulty in viewing these should not participate in the study. I would then ask for names and phone numbers of persons who would like to volunteer as participants.

From these lists obtained at speaking engagements, I selected my subjects. I would call people and once again remind them that they would be asked to look at pornographic photographs. Anyone who showed hesitancy or overeagerness I rejected as a subject. I also rejected individuals who had heard about my study and called to ask me if they could be a part of it. I wanted my subjects to be highly interested but not overly enthusiastic or simply motivated by a desire to look at pornographic pictures.

I had about 280 volunteers whom I considered viable subjects. From these, using age as the criterion, I selected a sampling of two hundred. In the majority of recent research done on sexuality and other topics, college students are used as subjects. This is because: (1) most experiments are conducted in college or university settings, and (2) college students are usually in need of the money they can obtain from participating in an experimental study.

I did not feel comfortable using college students in my study on sexual preferences, nor even persons in their very early twenties. I felt that the ages of eighteen to twenty-five were unrealistic for what I was trying to determine. The process of learning one's sexual preferences seems to require some duration of sexual relationship with one person. Most people who are involved in an active and by and large monogamous sexual relationship usually fall into a more mature range.

I found that the persons who had volunteered to participate in my study ranged in age from twenty-one to sixty-five. I decided to use subjects whose ages were between twenty-seven and forty-nine because I felt that these persons would have enough sexual experience not to consider sexual activity novel and innovative. Also, people in this age range are struggling with a variety of issues that I planned to address in this book.

I made no attempt in the study to determine if, for example, the twenty-seven-to-thirty-five-year-olds would demonstrate preferences for sexual activities that were radically different from or similar to those chosen by the thirty-five-to-forty- or the forty-to-forty-nine-year-olds. There is a need for further research in the area of developmental issues of mid-life sexuality.

I would speculate that, had I used either much younger (age eighteen to twenty-five) or much older (age fifty-five to seventy) subjects, both groups would have tended to choose much more conventional and traditional forms of preferences for sexual activity than those actually chosen in my sampling. Younger people are often conditioned to the experiences they have had as adolescents, which tend to be heavy petting and conventional ("missionary") intercourse. Older people tend to respond to what they think may be viewed as socially acceptable and appropriate. Again, this is my own speculation, and I think an area for further research and exploration.

My subjects were selected from professional, academic, and social organizations. They were all middle-class whites, some married and some single. They came from a variety of ethnic backgrounds: French, Italian, English, and others. All were, however, second- or third-generation Americans and well homogenized into the American culture. All came from a Judeo-Christian religious background. They were basically professional and white-collar workers or, in the case of many of the unemployed females, wives of professional and white-collar workers.

All of the subjects resided within the Chicago metropolitan area and were well acclimated to urban life-styles. I did not specifically determine their level of education or income.

This is admittedly a homogeneous sampling. I would agree with those who might question the similarity of class, occupational, racial, ethnic, and religious background in my subjects that there is a need for further research on different samplings: blue-collar workers, specific ethnic groups, a variety of educational levels, and others. It is my speculation that, given what is being determined in this study—adult male and female preferences for sexual activity as measured by the excitatory value of pornographic pictures—significant variations would not be found.

We are defining what looks like it would most deeply excite or engage the adult male and female sexual impulse, and this, I believe, is more a matter of physical and psychological rather than cultural or economic functions. I should also state that my subjects were heterosexual by their own admission. A study most definitely should be done on those sexual preferences for activities that are meaningful and important to the gay community.

After this careful determination and screening, I now had two hundred subjects ready to participate in my study. I had already decided what medium and methodology I would use, as I was following the Brady-Levitt model of presenting pornographic photographs to develop a selective rating system. I had explored the possibility of using as a testing medium various alternatives to the pornographic photographs —such as motion pictures, interviews, a self-testing questionnaire, surrogates, and erotic literature—but I kept coming up with limitations for each one.

Motion pictures are often used in clinical settings for teaching techniques and for desensitizing people who have some difficulty with sexual attitudes and performance. I felt that for my study, motion pictures might confound the subjects by asking them to concentrate on rapid action rather than on their own responses. I had to consider the element of time. With photographs, people could take their time in looking at them. The time element in motion pictures limits the individual's ability to make calculated perceptual choices. With photographs, the subjects could return to any one they wanted to reconsider and, if they chose, change their decisions.

Another possible alternative to the photographs was to interview each subject. This method can be used very productively for individual counseling and for sexual research involving couples and their actual experiences as opposed to sexual stimuli and/or fantasy. I used interviews, in fact, for the follow-up work to my study in attempting to determine whether or not the study itself changed sexual behavior in couples.

For the study itself, however, I felt that I would have to deal with the same set of problems that Kinsey did when he conducted his interview research. He found that he actually had to train his interviewees in the process of responding to questions in order to achieve valid responses. In the interview situation, the subject quite typically feels embarrassed, uncomfortable, and somewhat intimidated because of being put "on the spot."

Also, the interviewee can interpret any body language or gesture of the interviewer as judgmental. The person may change an initial response in order to comply with whatever feelings he or she is projecting onto the interviewer. Subjects are usually very interested in pleasing the interviewer and they will look to him or her for clues, which may in turn influence and determine responses.

A study was once conducted to determine whether or not an individual liked apples or oranges. In this stated attempt to assess fruit preferences, interviewers were actually attempting to see if they could influence their subjects' responses by giving both verbal and nonverbal feedback. I did not want my subjects to determine their sexual preferences by whether or not I felt like scratching my nose at any particular moment.

The self-testing questionnaire was another option I had available, and one that I quickly rejected. For the purpose of the study, I needed a medium that would provide my subjects with enough erotically charged stimulation to arouse them to a point of wanting to make specific choices about the depiction of themes. A self-testing questionnaire might allow them to create fantasies and/or experiences in their own words, but it could in no way control the level of stimulation needed for them to make the necessary choices.

An alternative that was, in my judgment, theoretically yet not practically or ethically possible, was the use of sexual surrogates. This method would have required each subject's participation with a surrogate in each of the nineteen sexual activities in order to determine which they enjoyed most. This would surely make subjects highly self-conscious, uncomfortable, and confused.

Masters and Johnson advocated the use of surrogates for therapeutic treatment of persons suffering from sexual dysfunction. While controversial for treatment, I think it would be considered unethical for purposes of a study like mine. One can immediately see the kinds of drawbacks inherent in this kind of experimental treatment, the most obvious being the moral restrictions and evaluations that most people would place upon it.

A final alternative to photographs is the use of erotic literature to determine sexual preferences. Studies have shown that people do become aroused by reading erotic material and that they do respond.[12] For the type of research I was conducting, erotic literature would have been my second choice. The basic difficulty with this medium is that it leaves a lot open to the imagination and may, therefore, result in modified statistical results in a study attempting to measure individual responses to set themes.

Photographs introduce limitations on the presentation of sexual themes in a way that literature does not. All my subjects were responding to the same visual media; they were seeing what was in front of them rather than configurations of their own imaginations. With reading materials, they could modify how the persons looked, what settings they were in, and how intensely they were responding to one another.

When we come to the self-test of sexual preference in the next chapter, we will employ written erotic descriptions as an alternative to the photographs that for obvious reasons could not be published in this book. Readers will be able to follow a model as close as possible to that used by my subjects in the original experiment. They will, obviously, however, be responding to written words rather than photographic representations of the sexual themes.

There is, of course, a very important difference between the experience of responding to photographs and the experience of responding to words. The photographs are completely static and frozen in time while the word pictures are full of action and movement. There is an obvious difference in responding to a picture of one suspended moment of penetration and reading a description of a male thrusting his penis in and out of a female vagina. The use of erotic material for the self-test is, however, the closest proximation to the medium model of the study that I can offer readers of this book.

I feel this is justified because it is important that the reader have an opportunity to discover his or her own sexual preferences. I am trying to allow the reader to get as close to the subjects' actual experience of participation as possible.

One of the most important questions involved in the choice of photographs as a medium was the selection of specific photographs for viewing. As I was following the Brady-Levitt model of providing three photographs to represent each of nineteen sexual themes, I needed a total of fifty-seven photographs. I needed to use three photographs for each theme in order to statistically estimate the reliability of the rating of the themes.[13] Another purpose in using three photographs of each theme (and using three erotic descriptions of each theme in the self-test which follows) is to try to insure that the reader is not measuring the theme on the basis of a specific response to a particular individual (as pictured or as described) or situation. Often I am asked why there are only nineteen themes in the study and why these particular themes were chosen.

In using the exact sexual themes presented in the original study, I was relying on the reliability factor that had been determined there. This is not to say that more and other themes could not have been employed. In order to simplify statistical validity of my study, however, I chose to repeat the sexual themes validated by Brady and Levitt.

I found the fifty-seven photographs by searching through a variety of pornographic materials. Of two hundred and fifty photographs, the final fifty-seven were chosen by a panel of four judges who reviewed each of them and determined those that were most representative of the sexual themes. Choices were made on the basis of the youthful attractiveness of individuals in the photographs, the contemporaneity in clothing and hairstyle, in furniture of the setting, and in rough equivalence in the degree of nudity and the positions of the participants.

The method by which the subjects actually viewed and ranked the photographs was uniform. I asked each subject to choose a time of day for coming to the research center when they would not feel rushed. The subjects could make appointments anytime between 9:00 A.M. and 9:00 P.M. I wanted to make sure that they would be comfortable with their chosen times and feel relaxed.

The setting for the experimental treatment was a room furnished as a comfortable den, with earth tones and soft lighting. Each subject arrived independently at the center and took the experimental treatment alone in this room. I accompanied them to the room, informed them of the scientific purpose of the study, and assured them of their anonymity.

I also told them that there were two parts to the study. They were first to view the photographs and rate them in order of preference. Then they would call me to the room and I would remove the photographs so that they could take the second portion of the study, in which they were asked to predict what their own sex and the other sex would prefer.

Seated at a table supplied with pencils, a rating sheet, and fifty-seven manila envelopes, each containing a single photograph, subjects were asked to sign the following consent form:

> I am totally aware of the fact that the photographs I will be viewing are pornographic in nature, and I do hereby consent voluntarily.

At this point, I would ask the subject if he or she had any questions and, if not, I would leave the room. Each person was presented with the following instruction:

> Your task is to rate each of the photographs according to the degree to which you find it sexually stimulating. Give each photograph a numerical rating on the scale below. A rating of 0 means that the photograph is not at all sexually stimulating to you. A rating of 5 means that the photograph is very highly stimulating. Ratings of 1, 2, 3, and 4 mean varying degrees of erotic value in ascending order. Thus a rating of 4 means that the photograph is less stimulating than 5 but more stimulating than 3, and so forth.

In general, women took about forty-five to fifty minutes to view the fifty-seven photographs, or fifty-three seconds for each photograph. Men took less time, usually completing the first portion of the experiment in thirty to thirty-five minutes, or approximately thirty-seven seconds for each photograph.

The photographs did not appear in any set order, and each subject viewed them in a different order from the previous subject. The purpose of shuffling the photographs after each had viewed them was to make the study more random. The subjects were given no time limit, and were told that they could go back to any of the photographs for subsequent viewing.

After looking at each photograph, rating it on the designated scale, and returning each photograph to its proper manila envelope, subjects were told to place their rating sheets face down on the table and to call me back into the room.

It was interesting to me that the subjects seemed to require some time to compose themselves after viewing these photographs. It usually took a while before eye contact with me was established when I entered the room to explain to them the second portion of the study, which asked them without benefit of photographic stimulus to predict the sexual preferences of other members of their own and the opposite sex.

For this second part, I showed them a sheet that listed the nineteen themes, and explained that although they had been viewing fifty-seven photographs, they had actually been considering only nineteen themes. I asked the subjects to read through the themes to determine whether or not they had any questions about the meaning of the words that were representative descriptions of the photographs they had just viewed.

Most subjects had no difficulty at all connecting the themes with the photographs. I then would ask them to perform what was admittedly a difficult task. They were given these specific instructions:

> Your task is to rank the nineteen themes, as you believe other females (Sheet A) and other males (Sheet B) would rank them. Please rank them on a 1–19 scale, with 1 being the most sexually stimulating theme to other females and other males, and 19 the least sexually stimulating theme. You are to use the entire range of numbers from 1 to 19.

After reading these instructions, subjects would often ask, "What am I basing this on?" My answer was that their predictions were based on a combination of all the various input they had received from the media, conversations with friends, their own fantasies, basically everything that had filtered into and through them about sexual preferences.

If the subjects had no more questions or comments, I would then leave the room to allow them to complete the second portion of the task. I removed the photographs at this time, so subjects would not be tempted to refer to the actual pictures. After finishing the ranking of predictions, subjects would then call me back into the room. Both men and women usually completed this task within a twenty-minute period.

This time when I returned to the room there was much better eye contact and much less embarrassment. The subjects were now addressing themselves to other people's preferences and felt less self-conscious. At this time I would give the subjects an opportunity to ask questions and/or make comments. I felt a sense of professional responsibility to help them close this experience. Also, I was naturally interested in any input that would advance my own information about sexual preferences.

Many women commented on the fact that this was the first time they had ever viewed pornographic photographs and that they found it to be very arousing. Most of the women who admitted that the photographs were sexually stimulating also stated that they felt they had been somewhat "cheated" in never before having had this kind of material available to them.

Men were as talkative as women after completing the predictions portion of the study. Their major interest was in the results, which, of course, I had yet to determine. There were many questions concerning what the study would be used for, and I sensed that both men and women subjects wanted to feel that they had made an important contribution.

Subjects were told to call me if they had any further information, questions, or comments. I received numerous follow-up calls, most of them reports that viewing the photographs had so aroused the subjects that their sexual activity during the twenty-four-hour period following participation was markedly increased. By showing that the photographs actually increased sexual behavior, this news further confirmed for me the validity of the methodology.

It seems appropriate to comment briefly on some of the statistical implications of the study. After my subjects' responses and predictions were completed, they were gathered together for analysis and interpretation. Several scientific statistical methods were used to determine issues such as: Was there a significant difference between thematic preferences? I wanted to ascertain whether ratings between the first ranked theme and the second or the second and the fourth had any considerable variations.

In the appendix the reader will have the opportunity to see the differences in the ratings between themes. There is more of a marked difference, for example, between themes 1 and 9 than there is between themes 1 and 3. Statistical tests showed that there were no significant differences in terms of average *ratings,* which are determined on a 0 to 5 scale (see Tables A and B) for many themes discussed throughout the book. There is, however, a difference of levels of arousal in the *rankings,* which are determined on a 1 to 19 scale (see Table C) of the themes.

It is of further interest that every theme, regardless of content, had a mean rating greater than 0 on a 0-to-5 scale. This means that all themes had some sexually stimulating value to the subjects. In general, the consistency of the ratings was very high, and the differences among mean ratings appear to be statistically significant but numerically trivial. This profile follows that established in the original Brady-Levitt study.[14]

Another issue verified by the statistical measurement of a t-test (a test that examines two sample means and compares them to determine differences or similarities) was the comparison of female and male average ratings of preference for the nineteen sexual themes. It revealed that thirteen of the nineteen themes were significantly different. This test proved statistically that there were degrees of difference between what the males and females found to be sexually stimulating.

A question that could have bearing on the reliability of the study is whether the photographs in each set were rated equivalently. Large correlations suggest that the common element, the depicted sexual activity, is the paramount factor upon which ratings were based. Any discrepancy introduced by extraneous factors was minimal.

The single most revealing measure of reliability in this case was an analysis of the consistency of each subject in making ratings of the different themes across the three sets of photographs. This was assessed by correlating subjects' ratings of the three sets of each of the nineteen themes with each other. A perfect correlation in this type of statistical analysis would be 1.00.

The average inter-correlation (on a scale of 1.00) for sets of photographs for female subjects was .94 while for males it was .90, both obviously very high correlations. It is evident that the subjects manifested a high degree of consistency and continuity when rating the three different photographs that depicted each theme and therefore were not simply reacting to the variables such as the attractiveness of the subjects depicted.

A Spearman rank-order-correlation coefficient (a method which helps to measure correlations between scores) was used to determine both individual and group correlations in answering the question of how accurately females and males could estimate their own sexual preferences as well as those of the opposite sex. The results indicated that subjects were slightly more accurate as a group than individually.

For example, the individual correlation for females' ability to estimate other females' sexual preferences was .57. The group correlation for females' ability to predict same sex preference was .86. The average correlation for individual males' ability to estimate other males' preference was .74, while the group correlation was .82.

Before moving on, I would like to comment on the relatively small, and, in terms of the total population, relatively unrepresentative sample used to determine this information. The largest sample base for a sexual study was in that undertaken by Kinsey, who collected data on nearly eight thousand females for his study on *Sexual Behavior in the Human Female.* Such an undertaking has never been attempted or repeated on a similar grandiose scale. I do not pretend that my study compares to the vast research and interpretation of results conducted there.

I do, however, think that my study is valid. If, for example, one looks at *Psychological Abstracts,* it becomes clear that the majority of scientific experiments performed in the area of sexuality employ a small and somewhat unrepresentative sampling.

As a case in point, Brady and Levitt used only sixty-eight subjects, all male, ranging from twenty-one to thirty-two years of age, with a mean age of 23.9. They broke their subjects down into married and unmarried, Protestant and Catholic. They did not determine racial, ethnic, or economic differences of their subjects, and one might question the universality of their sampling. Their study, however, is a scientifically validated and professionally respected experiment.

Very frequently clinical applications for patient treatment are based on experimental studies that use as small a sampling as ten or twenty people.[15] This is possible because we are able, from a small sampling, to make some larger generalizations about the entire population. The very fact that we label them as generalizations means that there are, of course, exceptions and variations.

In my own study, there appeared to be a consensus about what themes males and females respectively found to be sexually stimulating. This does not mean that some readers will not differ with both the results of the data and perhaps, my interpretation of the data.

It is also quite possible that other theorists in the field of psychology might examine the results of the study and offer quite new and different interpretations. I myself could obviously not cover in depth all of the reasons why particular choices among themes were made. I interpreted the results based on my own eclectic approach to the dynamics of human behavior and, from my knowledge of the field, my clinical experience, and what I believe to be true about general principles of human sexuality. I am open to whatever contributions, supplementary or contradictory, other professionals may offer.

In the presentation of this study, I do not pretend to offer a definitive philosophy of truth about male and female sexual responses and preferences. I am merely offering my findings and my personal perceptions based on extensive research, empirical experimentation, and clinical experience. It is my hope that other sex researchers as well as lay leaders will find food for thought here as well as some insights and, I hope, guidance.

We are now left with the obvious questions: What *were* the results? What *do* females and males most enjoy sexually? This information will be presented in Chapter 4.

But before you learn the results of the Kahn Study,

perhaps you'd like to try to simulate the laboratory experience of my study subjects, using words instead of pictures, and thereby determine your own, perhaps incompletely perceived or barely recognized, sexual preference using the self-testing guide in the next chapter.

3 Determining Your Own Sexual Preferences

READERS of this book may never have thought to ask themselves, much less their partners, what sexual activities they most prefer. And if readers have asked themselves they probably had no notion how to determine such a thing beyond searching their own memories. I am reminded of the person who never having really looked at a painting by Picasso rejects it out of hand, saying: "I don't know much about painting, but I know what I like." It is quite possible that, through the self-test that follows, readers may discover new evidence and learn that they like something they didn't previously know existed.

Volunteers who participated in the study certainly expressed this eagerness to learn something new about themselves. They wanted to check out their own responses against a scientific model of sexual preferences. The point here is that even though we may think that we know our own sexual preferences, it is quite possible that we don't, and that we need some help in making new and exciting discoveries about ourselves and others.

For this reason, I feel it is important to provide readers with an opportunity to explore their preferences through the self-test. By taking this test, independently and removed from a particular problem or sexual situation, the reader can make some discoveries about him- or herself as well as compare his or her results against the surprising and unexpected results presented in Chapter Four.

The erotic material that follows will, I hope, serve the purpose that the pornographic photographs served in the study—to arouse the participant. Since I could not reproduce these photographs in the book, I am providing the reader with this alternative. It is important to repeat that the erotic descriptions do differ from photographs in that they move through time and possess a great deal of action, whereas the photographs suspend time and represent stopped action.

Readers who have enjoyed erotic material in the past may recall the experience of heightened sexual response—increase in heartbeat, rapidity of breathing, facial flush, swelling and arousal of the genitals. Usually there is no consequence to this arousal other than sexual stimulation. In providing erotic descriptions of the sexual themes used in my study, I am giving the reader an opportunity to use this sexual stimulation for the purpose of self-discovery and direction.

As you read and notice your responses, please respect and acknowledge them as material that can be used for self-awareness and for future reference. By reading, responding to and ranking the sexual themes in the first self-test, you will be able to, perhaps for the first time, learn what forms of sexual activity you actually prefer. These may or may not differ from those forms that you presently engage in. It is essential that you become actively involved in the descriptions and that you take both the words and your responses to them seriously.

Also, it may help to supplement the material with some of your own choices in erotic reading. A good literary source for this purpose would be Anaïs Nin's erotica: *Delta of Venus* and *Little Birds.* For visual stimulation, you may look into erotic art. Almost all the great artists, at one time in their development, explored erotica, and this material is generally available at bookstores and libraries.

When you take the self-test, make sure that you choose a time of day when you are relaxed and free from pressures. Be dressed comfortably, and indulge in any relaxing activities that you feel will most contribute to your ability to enjoy and respond to the descriptions. These might include a warm bath, soft music, deep breathing, a very comfortable chair, sofa, or bed.

I strongly suggest that you do this while you are alone. This way you will not feel required to disguise or elaborate responses in consideration of your partner. There is no reason why you cannot share this experience after you have completed the ranking, but the involvement of another person in the initial testing may tend to modify and qualify your responses. The fundamental key to taking this test is to allow yourself to be fully open for sexual arousal that will stimulate you to make test choices, without guilt, pressure, or fear of either positive or negative criticism.

The following pages present descriptive samplings of the nineteen sexual themes used in the study. The numbered sexual themes are listed with instructions; each corresponds to one of the descriptive passages. There is no need to read the samplings in any specific order; it is probably best if you read them in a random sequence and then make your choices.

Please read the descriptions carefully and rank the themes according to the degree to which you find them sexually stimulating, as indicated in the instructions. After completing your own ranking sheet, use the appropriate sheets to rank the same themes as you believe other females and other males would rank them.

This self-instruction is for you. I am not attempting to secure more data from reader responses. I am attempting to give you an opportunity that you will find helpful and, hopefully, growth-producing.

SEXUAL THEMES

What Do You Prefer Sexually?

Instructions:

Referring to the descriptions in this chapter and your own fantasies, your task is to rank the 19 themes presented below in terms of how sexually stimulating you find them to be. Please rank them on a 1-to-19 scale, 1 being the most sexually stimulating theme, and 19 the least sexually stimulating theme.

Themes

Heterosexual intercourse, male on top of female	______
Heterosexual intercourse, female on top of male	______
Heterosexual petting, both nude	______
Heterosexual petting, both partially clad	______
Heterosexual fellatio: oral sex, female on male	______
Nude female	______
Heterosexual cunnilingus: oral sex, male on female	______
Female masturbation	______
Triad: two males and one female joined together and engaged in coitus and/or oral-genital activity	______
Partially clad female	______
Homosexual cunnilingus	______
Homosexual petting, female	______
Sadomasochism, male on female	______
Homosexual fellatio	______
Sadomasochism, female on male	______
Male masturbation	______
Homosexual anal intercourse	______
Nude male	______
Partially clad male	______

THE KAHN REPORT ON SEXUAL PREFERENCES

What Do You Think Women Prefer Sexually?

Instructions:

Your task is to rank the 19 themes presented below in terms of how sexually stimulating you think women would find them. (If you are a female, please consider what you think heterosexual females prefer.) Please rank them on a 1-to-19 scale, 1 being the most sexually stimulating theme to women, and 19 being the least sexually stimulating to women.

Themes

Heterosexual intercourse, male on top of female	______
Heterosexual intercourse, female on top of male	______
Heterosexual petting, both nude	______
Heterosexual petting, both partially clad	______
Heterosexual fellatio: oral sex, female on male	______
Nude female	______
Heterosexual cunnilingus: oral sex, male on female	______
Female masturbation	______
Triad: two males and one female joined together and engaged in coitus and/or oral-genital activity	______
Partially clad female	______
Homosexual cunnilingus	______
Homosexual petting, female	______
Sadomasochism, male on female	______
Homosexual fellatio	______
Sadomasochism, female on male	______
Male masturbation	______
Homosexual anal intercourse	______
Nude male	______
Partially clad male	______

What Do You Think Men Prefer Sexually?

Instructions:

Your task is to rank the 19 themes presented below in terms of how sexually stimulating you think men would find them. (If you are a male, please consider what you think *other* heterosexual males prefer.) Please rank them on a 1-to-19 scale, 1 being the most sexually stimulating theme to men, and 19 being the least sexually stimulating to men.

Themes

Heterosexual intercourse, male on top of female	______
Heterosexual intercourse, female on top of male	______
Heterosexual petting, both nude	______
Heterosexual petting, both partially clad	______
Heterosexual fellatio: oral sex, female on male	______
Nude female	______
Heterosexual cunnilingus: oral sex, male on female	______
Female masturbation	______
Triad: two males and one female joined together and engaged in coitus and/or oral-genital activity	______
Partially clad female	______
Homosexual cunnilingus	______
Homosexual petting, female	______
Sadomasochism, male on female	______
Homosexual fellatio	______
Sadomasochism, female on male	______
Male masturbation	______
Homosexual anal intercourse	______
Nude male	______
Partially clad male	______

Heterosexual Intercourse, Male on Top of Female

A. Lisa lies sleeping on the chaise longue. Her straight brown hair falls in soft waves around her neck. Her body is stretched out so that one arm is flung above her head. Her skin, soft and glowing, is exposed to the strength of the midday sun streaming through the west window. Erik comes into the room and looks at her. He immediately feels himself becoming hard. He undresses and approaches the chaise longue. On a nearby table he sees a single, long-stemmed, red carnation in a slender blue vase. He picks up the flower and, very gently, begins to run it up and down the inside of Lisa's smooth, white thigh waking her. Lisa looks up and smiles. With the carnation, Erik lightly touches the dark pubic hair curling around Lisa's vagina. She tenses her body and arches her back. Without a word, Erik places the carnation beside her, hooks his arms under her knees so that her buttocks rise high in the air, and enters her. Lisa moans and begins to move her full hips in circles around his huge, hardened penis. Erik sighs and breathes heavily. Lisa clasps her ankles around his waist, throws back her head, and begs him to thrust hard into her.

B. A beautiful young woman is dressing for her lover. She has bought a set of bra and panties, flesh-colored and trimmed with lace. She has a full, woman's body, the legs nicely curved, the shapely ass rounded. She stands waiting for him as he climbs the stairs to her apartment. He is lean and muscular with an intense, sensual face. He enters the door and looks at her. He orders her to lie down on the floor. Unzipping the fly to his jeans, he stares at her breasts through the flesh-colored nylon and lowers himself upon her. Lifting the crotch of the bikini panties, he looks at the light, reddish pubic hair, the vagina, he sees the tiny clitoris. His penis is bulging from the opening in his pants, and he presses it against her leg as he covers her open mouth with his own. She reaches down and puts his penis inside her. He props himself up with his hands flat on the floor and begins to thrust deep inside her, with long strokes that cause her to shake, to moan.

C. Dora is sitting propped up with pillows on the bed. Her legs are open and stretched out in a V in front of her. She is nude, and her full, heavy breasts sway slightly as she strokes and fondles them. James is in the room watching her. He likes to see her caress herself. He begins to rub his penis and it stretches out toward Dora, who loves the sight of the large, smooth penis. She begins to move her hands down toward her stomach and thighs. James approaches her, and she reaches out to encircle his penis with her hand. James takes her nipples in his fingers and twirls them around. With her legs still apart, Dora moves downward on the bed. James clasps her ankles and lifts them high so that he can see the opening of the vagina. Placing his thighs against her buttocks, he puts his penis against her. Dora grabs him close to her breasts as he plunges inside her.

Heterosexual Intercourse, Female on Top of Male

A. Frank is lying nude on the bed as she comes in from the pool. She removes her wet bikini as soon as she steps inside the room. He watches her and becomes excited by her lithe, tanned body, the breasts and pelvis dramatically white against her young, golden flesh. She glances over at him and sees that his penis is huge, its head pointing toward the ceiling. Silently, she walks toward the bed, and, with her back facing him, mounts his penis. Throwing back her head, she begins moving up and down upon him, her arms stretched back, feeling his tensing, taut body.

B. In the small alcove adjoining the bedroom, there is a wooden chair, with a high back, sturdy arms, and a red velvet cushion. Next to it, an antique table holding a bouquet of flowers. The couple had undressed in the living room and were on their way to the bedroom when she orders him to sit down on the chair. He smiles at her and sits down as she starts to rub his penis with her right hand. With her left, she takes his hand and places it on one of her breasts. He begins to fondle it and then to suck on it. She offers him the other breast and as he starts to nibble and suck, she straddles him, holding herself up with her hands on the arms of the chair. His penis, long and hard, securely inside her, she begins to move up and down, her legs spilling over and swinging from the sides of the chair.

C. The woman is sitting on top of the man, with her back facing him. The man's whole body is taut and tense. She raises herself to the top of his penis, almost removing herself from it, and then plunges quickly down upon it. The man moans with each of her downward strokes. She turns around and mounts him face to face. As he watches her breasts sway with her up and downward movement, he raises himself toward her, suckles at a breast, and comes.

Heterosexual Petting, Both Nude

A. George and Julie had spent the afternoon sailing. It was a gorgeous day—sun sparkling on the deep green water, the sky astonishingly blue. George had packed a delicious lunch, thin slices of smoked salmon, cream cheese rolled up on a delicate roll, a bottle of chilled Chablis. After lunch he spreads out a blue comforter on the deck and takes off his swimsuit. He walks over to Julie and removes the straw sun hat she wore to cover her thick mane of red hair. As her hair tumbles over her shoulders, he unzips her shorts and takes off her blouse. She wears no bra. Easing her onto the blue comforter, he begins to rub her legs. Julie feels the hot sun on her body, reaches over for a sip of wine, and then lets George explore her mouth. They kiss for a long while, as his hands explore her breasts and thighs and her hands roam over his back and buttocks. They remain together nude, kissing and touching until sundown.

B. He is anxious to get home to her. In the elevator in the high-rise apartment, he thinks about her and the evening ahead. As he puts the key in the lock and opens the door, he calls out. She answers from the bedroom. He throws his briefcase on the hall table and quickly steps out of his clothes. Nearing the open door to the bedroom, he sees her stretched out nude on a red divan with small, brightly colored pillows surrounding her. He walks to the side of the divan and, without a word, she encircles his erect penis with her left hand. As she begins to move her hand up and down, he reaches down to touch her clitoris. Soon they are side by side on the divan, their mouths together, her hand still on his penis, his fingers moving upward inside her vagina.

C. Early morning. Still two hours before the alarm would go off. They are both between sleep and waking, her back to him, his arms circle around her waist. He feels her stir, and her movement makes him aware of his penis, slowly awakening to the feel of her flesh. He moves his hands upward to fondle her breasts. She moves her hand down to his enlarging penis. Delighted to find him so erect, she slowly turns her body toward his, as his hands remain on her breasts. Side by side they begin kissing, first short kisses, which then grow longer and longer.

Heterosexual Petting, Both Partially Clad

A. Monica is wearing only a pair of bikini pants. She is stretching over the bed when her lover walks into the room. He is wearing white pants, no shirt. He likes the way her bottom moves as she tries to straighten the covers on the far side of the bed. Her hair is long, full, and curly as it bounces against her back. He walks over to her and yanks her bikini pants. Startled, she turns toward him. He grabs her arms and pulls her up to him. She feels the bulge inside his pants. As he is putting his hands into the back of her pants, she unzips his fly. He begins to pull down the silk bikini and clasps her small, rounded buttocks with his large hands. She puts her hands into his unzipped pants and begins sliding them down his hips until his pubic hair is exposed. He moves his chest against her breasts as he bends his head and kisses her shoulder.

B. The young woman wears a light, sleeveless, summer dress, and she is sitting on the end of a large, comfortable sofa. Her long blond hair is freshly washed and shining in the light of one lamp. The man is fully dressed and sits down beside her. Slowly he rubs his hand up and down her thigh until her dress begins to move upward. When his hand reaches her crotch, he feels soft nylon panties. Her mouth is open and she begins to breathe more heavily. He slides the panties down her thighs. She lifts her left leg and reaches down to slide the panties over her black high-heeled shoes. As his fingers explore the light, soft hair on her genitals, she begins to unbuckle his belt. He moves his face downward toward hers.

C. A large, four-poster bed. Deep, rich satin quilt. A woman with a sheer, short nighty trimmed in black lace. It is a hot night, and the man enters the room dressed in a short-sleeved shirt and light pants. The woman is rubbing herself with a scented lotion. She smoothes it over her arms and neck. Through the sheer nightie, he can see the swell of her breasts, the hard nipples. He walks toward her and she puts the lotion down on a bedside table. He sees that she is wearing very sheer panties under the nightie. Putting his hand inside the panties, he bends down to her and puts his face against her breasts. She lifts the nightie so he can lick her nipples. Throwing her head back, she grabs his neck and begins to unbutton his shirt.

Heterosexual Fellatio: Oral Sex, Female on Male

A. The man is large and muscular, with dark hair covering his chest and legs. He is stretched out nude on a purple couch, his hands behind his head, which is propped up on a pillow. The woman comes into the room. She is darkly blonde, with small, rounded breasts and lovely long, slender legs. She walks over to the couch and sits down beside the man. She sees that he is only slightly erect. Standing up, she walks to the end of the couch and kneels over his knees. She takes the pins out of her blond hair and lets it fall over his chest and stomach. Then she takes his penis in her right hand and inserts it into her open mouth. She moves her tongue up and down, to the side, and up and down again. The man does not alter the position of his head or hands. She continues to move her tongue on his penis, and soon he begins to writhe. She applies more pressure with her hand and mouth, and he becomes extremely erect. His hips move along with her mouth. When she can feel that he is ready to come, she raises her head and looks at him.

B. She is lying on her back on a green fur rug. She has large eyes, a straight nose, and a full, sensuous mouth. She wears no clothes. The man who is watching her is of medium height, with dark-reddish hair, large shoulders and chest, a slim waist. He notices her very full breasts, her shapely legs. Erect and nude, he walks over to the rug and kneels at the edge of it. She slids her feet, ankles, and calves through his thighs until he is straddled over her. Then she grasps his buttocks and moves him up toward her. When his penis is close enough to her, she opens her mouth and slides her tongue over the top. He closes his eyes and she takes his full penis into her mouth and begins sucking hard on it. She moves so that his testicles will fall on her breasts and then, with her mouth still encircling his penis, she begins to squeeze his buttocks.

C. He is seated on a chair nude. The woman is standing near the chair. She is nude from the waist up. She is looking at the man's penis. He grabs her hand and propels her so that she is standing directly in front of him. He reaches up to stroke her breasts, and then places his arms on her shoulders, pulling her downward so that she is kneeling in front of him. She is fascinated by the size of his penis. Gently, he places his left hand on her head and pulls her so close that she can easily reach his penis with her mouth. Grasping his testicles with her right hand, she puts her mouth over his erect penis. He moves her head in and out, in and out until he is ready to come.

Nude Female

A. A voluptuous young Scandinavian woman is sitting on a yellow towel spread out on grass. Her arms are stretched behind her and her head is thrown back so that her face and neck are facing the sun. Her breasts are firm, full, and unusually large. Her nipples are taut. She wears nothing but a pearl choker and a long gold chain that falls gently between her breasts. She is well tanned, and her breasts and pelvic area are white against the golden flesh. Her right leg is slightly lifted, her legs gently spread apart. Her dark-blond hair falls down to the towel.

B. A dark Spanish woman with curly black hair is sprawled out on a brightly printed lounge chair. She is smiling and showing a dimple on her left cheek. She is looking down at her nude body with obvious pleasure. Her breasts are soft and rounded in the dim light. She is reaching toward the dark hair on her genitals. The flesh surrounding it is white. A red feather boa is on her right arm. She looks as if she might be waiting for a man.

C. Beside a curvaceous swimming pool stands an equally curvaceous young woman. She is well tanned and holding a long white terry-cloth towel. She is looking down at her moderately large breasts, which, like the area surrounding her pubic hair, appear as shocks of white against her deep golden body. Her brown hair is streaked by the sun and pulled back from her face.

Heterosexual Cunnilingus: Oral Sex, Male on Female

A. Jan and Len are walking toward the ocean parallel to the sensually molded sand dunes. Suddenly Jan feels Len's penis hard against her buttocks. He feels her breasts with his hands. Jan breaks free and runs toward the edge of the ocean, flinging her wraparound sun dress to her side. She turns to see Len unfasten his pants and leave them on the sand. He comes toward her. Jan lies down at the water's edge and slowly opens her legs to the water. Len walks into the water and faces her, grabbing her ankles and pulling them apart. Then he lies down on his stomach and puts his head between her legs. With brief, light kisses he explores her vagina. Jan shudders with delight and pleasure, feeling the water's cool movements and Len's hot mouth all at once. Then he runs his tongue up and down the glistening clitoris, tasting the salty liquids as Jan's buttocks tense and raise themselves into the air.

B. Barbara is sitting on a stool with her skirt up around her thighs. Dick is sketching her, drawing quick and easy lines on a drawing pad propped on his thighs as he sits cross-legged on the floor. "Pull your skirt up a little more, I want to get more of the upper thigh." Barbara smiles at him and quickly removes her panties, throwing them in his direction. She then sits back on the stool, pulls up her skirt so as to show her genitals, and opens up her legs. Dick begins to sketch the legs, then focuses upon the vagina. Barbara pulls apart the lips of her sex and shows him, by touching it with her finger, her clitoris. Dick asks her not to move and, putting aside his pad, walks over to her and kneels in front of the stool. Carefully removing her finger, so as not to lose the exact spot, he places his tongue directly on her and moves it up and down. Then he finds the hole of her vagina and thrusts his tongue in and out.

C. A woman is lying on a long wooden plank on the bare floor of a room. Her legs are raised up in the air, bent at the knees, which are spread apart. She is nude except for black straps wound around her calves and open-toed sandals on her feet. A man walks to the edge of the plank and removes all of his clothes. He bends down and grasps the woman's ankles. She sees that he is staring at her vagina. He moves forward and kisses the back of each thigh. She asks him to kiss her pubic hair. He puts his mouth lightly on the hair and grasps a dark wisp of a curl in his teeth. Then, putting his hands beneath her buttocks, he licks her clitoris, over and over, and begins thrusting his tongue into her vagina.

Female Masturbation

A. Linda brings a long mirror into the room and props it up against the bed. She sits down and opens her thighs to the mirror. With her fingers she opens up the lips of her genitals until she can see inside her vagina. She begins to explore it with one of her fingers until she is very wet. She thinks about her lover, Mark, of his hands and tongue upon her. She remembers what it felt like when his tongue touched her clitoris. Smoothly and gently she runs the tip of her finger over the clitoris. She pretends that Mark is there watching her. This excites her further, and she lies down on the floor, sideways so that she can see her whole body arch and writhe as she plays with her breasts, then puts one finger into her vagina and pushes in and out until she can see the look of pleasure and fulfillment in her face.

B. A man enters a bedroom holding a camera. A woman is lying on her stomach, nude, with her buttocks high in the air. Her face is turned from his as she looks at her ass in a mirror that is behind her. She sees the man and smiles at him. Looking down, she can see her own fingers as they rest against the hills of her buttocks, and she begins to move and sway. The man takes a picture of her and the flash startles her. He shows her the picture, which reveals her ass, her hands, her face, and himself, standing in front of her with the camera. She turns over so that her vagina and clitoris are clearly visible in the mirror. Moving her fingers in and out, she begins to circle her hips and, in a rotating motion, excites herself until, as she watches him prepare to take another picture, she comes.

C. Laura is lying on her bed. She is totally nude under the sheets. Her hands begin to move slowly over her breasts and her fingers commence to gently massage the nipples. Spontaneously, her legs spread apart. Her hips start rhythmically to move up and down while her head slowly rolls from side to side. She continues until she can no longer tolerate the sheet over her body. Everything must now be exposed. Her vagina aches to be touched. Her hand slides down across her damp stomach to her wet clitoris. Her fingers now explore every part of her vagina. They slide downward from the tip of her clitoris to the opening of her swelling vagina. The touching now takes on a large, circular rhythm. Her total body moves with the rubbing motion. She moves as the weak yet strong feeling through her body intensifies. The rhythm grows faster and faster. She is climbing and climbing. Her legs now become tight and tense. Suddenly, a charge of electricity flashes through her body.

Triad: Two Males and One Female Joined Together and Engaged in Coitus and/or Oral-Genital Activity

A. Helen had taken on two lovers. She usually sees them separately but tonight they are both coming to her. She always meets each of them in the nude, standing by her bed. Bryan arrives first. He has brought a bunch of wild daisies, which she placed in a vase near the bed. Then William joins them, bringing a bottle of chilled white wine. After each drinks a glass, the men undress. Bryan leads Helen to the bed and puts her down on her stomach. He rubs his penis all over the back of her thighs and ass until he is very hard. Helen reaches over and picks one of the daisies from the vase. Then she turns over and grabs Bryan's penis, wrapping the long green stem round the throbbing organ. William is fondling himself as he watches Bryan and Helen. He is becoming quite excited. He walks to the bed and spreads Helen's legs wide apart. Giving her small kisses on the inside of her thigh, he inserts one finger into her vagina. She is wet and ready. Lowering himself on top of her, he inserts his penis and begins pumping hard. Bryan positions himself directly above Helen at the other end of the bed so that she can suck his penis while petals of daisy fall soft and fast upon her breasts.

B. Sara has never felt anything like it. She wants only that it will never stop. She is in bed with two men, a dark-haired, muscular athlete and a light-haired poet. She has never met either of them before. The poet is speaking softly to her as he kisses and fondles her breasts. The athlete is spreading her legs and kissing the insides of her thighs. Sara is feeling such tingles and intense sensations that she is becoming unaware of what each man is doing. She feels her neck and breasts being delicately stroked and then another mouth begins suckling her nipples, first gently, then with greater pressure. A tongue runs up and down the inside of her thigh, and a finger is exploring the opening of her vagina. Then she is turned over and placed on her hands and knees while a tongue thrusts itself into her vagina and someone, from below her, begins licking her nipples.

C. Darin and Derek are fraternal twins. They are almost always attracted to the same women. After they had conferred on the specific charms and appeal of a woman, they approach her and ask her to go to bed with them. Usually, the women agree. After the first time, the women always come back. The twins like to have only one woman at a time with them, and they have established a particular pattern that appeals to them both. Darin undresses the woman slowly while Derek stands before her nude and shows her his magnificent penis, smooth and long. Then Darin takes the woman to the edge of the bed where he seats her and spreads her legs. Kneeling, Darin wets her vagina with his tongue, then stands and asks her to take his penis into her mouth. Derek, meanwhile, poses on his knees behind the woman and kisses her on the neck and shoulders. Then lying the woman down, Darin stretches above her in such a way so as to allow her to take his penis into her mouth, yet not interfere with Derek's exploration of her body with his tongue. At this point, the woman often begs to have a penis inside her. Then the twins take turns, penetrating and observing, giving the woman numerous and increasingly pleasurable orgasms. Only after she pleads exhaustion do each of the twins allow himself to come inside her.

Partially Clad Female

A. A woman wearing nothing from the waist up stands at the edge of a canopied bed and looks out from candid blue eyes. Her blond hair is pulled back gently, and her face is framed by two large, gold, looped earrings. Her breasts are remarkably beautiful. They are big, rounded, exquisitely shaped. She looks invitingly at you. Her mouth is slightly open. Her hands and nails are long and lovely. She looks like she wants to touch you, take you into that sensual, open mouth.

B. A fiery redheaded female stands at a window where light dazzles her hair and thighs. She wears only a sleeveless top, below the waist nothing. She stands so that her legs open just enough to reveal the dark curly hair on her genitals. Her breasts look full beneath the close-fitting top. She moves slightly, and tilts her hips toward you.

C. A sensual languid tropical day. The long blond hair sweeps downward onto a beautiful female body lying on a chaise longue. Adorning her large breasts is a silk halter, each breast covered by a large pink rose. Down the length of her, reaching as far as her vagina, is a long string of pink pearls. You can see her clitoris as she opens her legs slowly toward the sunlight streaking in on her.

Homosexual Cunnilingus

A. Two nude women are in a pool. The blonde one is lying on an air-filled raft, apparently asleep. Swimming up and down the length of the pool is a slender redhead, her hair flowing out behind her as she swims. No one else is in sight. Swimming toward the raft, the redhead swirls the raft so that she is able to fondle the young blonde woman's breasts. The blonde opens her eyes and smiles. The redhead moves them into shallow water and stands up beside the raft. She bends her head down to kiss the blonde on the mouth, a long, wet kiss, both tongues meeting. Slowly the redhead begins to kiss the blonde's neck, shoulder, breasts. She stops for a few moments at the breasts, nuzzling them, then moves downward. When she reaches the blond pubic hair, she feels a hand on her head pushing downward. Eagerly, the redhead spreads her lover's legs and glides her tongue up and down the clitoris.

B. In a small room Marion sits nude on a piano bench that has been placed against a wall. She has long brown hair, beautifully big breasts, long slender legs. She is waiting for someone. Another woman enters the room. Marion begins to rub her own arms, slowly, languidly. The other woman throws off a robe and, completely nude, walks over to the piano bench. She looks longingly at the big breasts and takes one in her hand. Marion grabs the hand and begins moving it back and forth, one breast, then the other. She then places her hands on her partner's shoulders and pulls her downward, so that she is kneeling at the bench, with her legs spread wide apart. Marion takes her partner's head in her hands and pulls it toward her vagina. Very quickly she feels a hot, moist tongue moving in and out of her vagina, up and down her clitoris. She throws her head back and moans.

C. Kathy does not move. Her legs are hanging over the side of the bed, her vagina is open. Cindy's head is between her two smooth legs and Kathy knows that soon she will feel the experienced tongue on her clitoris. Cindy's hands move up Kathy's thighs, enclasp the waist, and move on to the breasts. Kathy places her hands on Cindy's head and, with the gentlest of pressures, shows her where she wants to be licked, sucked, kissed. Then Cindy puts her tongue at the mouth of the vagina, just below the clitoris. She pushes it as far as it will go. Kathy feels Cindy's hands now on her buttocks, pushing in so that she feels that all of her sex is inside Cindy's mouth.

Homosexual Petting, Female

A. Softly and gently Joan begins to undress the young woman. She is wearing a low-cut dress with a short skirt. As she steps out of it Joan can see that she isn't wearing bra or underpants. Delighted, Joan begins immediately to fondle the young firm, supple breasts. They both become excited and the younger woman undresses her. Then, embracing tightly, they begin to explore each other's bodies. They are both slender, rounded, and soft. Joan turns the younger woman around so that she can cup the lovely breasts with her hands, and kiss the long, taut neck.

B. They had come home from the bar together. They had been dancing, and they wanted to continue to dance together in the nude. Each was excited about seeing the other's body. The brunette turns on the phonograph, a record they both enjoy. She begins to undress slowly, moving in time with the music. The blonde can see the large breasts sway, the round hips move. She too begins to undress and, when they are nude except for the necklaces and rings they both are wearing, they begin slow dancing. Clasped tightly and moving to the music, they can feel each other's breasts, play with each other's pubic hair. Soon they are kissing and rubbing each other's clitorises.

C. Steven loves to watch his women make love to each other. His two favorites, Maureen and Leila, know how to please Steven and themselves. Tonight Maureen comes out of the bathroom still wet and glistening from a hot bath. Leila is seated on the bed, wearing only an open lavendar robe that is short and ends just at the curve of her buttocks. She is the more feminine of the two, full in the breasts, quite slim in the waist, and attractively heavy in her hips. She spreads her legs so that Maureen can look inside her vagina. Maureen is tall and slim, with an angular beauty that appeals to photographers and artists. Stephen looks at her as she wraps a heavy purple towel around her body. He is seated on a chair in front of the bed so he can watch all of their movements. Maureen and Leila begin to kiss, their mouths open and wet. Maureen opens her towel and shows Leila her nude body. Leila bends forward and touches Maureen's clitoris, still wet from her recent bath. She feels it begin to stiffen and works her fingers more quickly. Maureen moans and takes Leila's heavy breasts into her hands, and they both fall back on the bed together. After a while, Steven moves toward them.

Sadomasochism, Male on Female

A. In a room with a tiger-striped couch, a dark brown rug, and an armless wooden chair two people stand looking at each other. The woman has short brown hair. The man is also dark, powerfully muscular. They are both nude. He starts to kiss her roughly on the mouth. She responds by grasping his erect penis in her hand and squeezing it tightly. He grabs one of her breasts and moves her toward the couch. Sitting her down, he reaches behind the couch and brings out a brown braided rope. He grasps her wrists and ties them with the rope. She tries to reach his penis with her hands, but can't. He is excited by this, and moves his penis toward her so she can hold it. He then sets the armless wood chair next to the couch and lifts her up to sit her on it. Holding her by the back of her knees, he raises her legs up in the air. She reaches up with her tied wrists and clasps her ankles with her hands. He then inserts his penis in her vagina. She throws her head back and eyes closed, mouth open, moans for more.

B. A woman is seated on a chair. She is wearing a short white silk robe and sheer black underpants. She has long red hair that reaches down to the silk belt on the robe. A man enters the room dressed in a shirt and pants. She looks up at him and asks for a cigarette. He takes out a rope and ties her wrists. She smiles and repeats her request. The man lights a cigarette and puts it in her mouth. He allows her to puff and then removes the cigarette. He asks if she wants more. Still smiling, she says yes as she watches him put out the cigarette. He then kneels by the chair and begins to open her robe so that he can see her breasts. Her nipples are taut. He quickly kisses each nipple and then grabs the woman's bound wrists.

He raises them in the air and swirls her around so that she is lying with her back on the seat of the chair, her arms stretched out over her head. He spreads her legs apart and puts his hand inside the sheer black underpants. He rubs her clitoris and feels her wet and moist. He asks if she wants some more. When she nods, he quickly slides his tongue up and down her clitoris and then inserts it in her vagina. She screams with delight.

C. Wearing only a long-sleeved black turtleneck a woman sits on an armless wood chair. A man comes in wearing only long black pants and carrying a riding whip in one hand, a black handkerchief and a rope in the other. The woman looks up and he greets her. He walks toward her and throws the riding whip at the side of the chair. He then gags her with the black handkerchief, asking her if she is comfortable. She nods and he lifts up the black turtleneck to expose her beautifully large breasts. They are pure white against the black wool. He then ties the rope around her waist so that she is bound to the chair. He begins to fondle her breasts, taking the nipples into his mouth. She murmurs and he puts his hand between her thighs. She is already wet. Standing up, close to the chair, he looks at her bound body, her firm breasts. Becoming erect, he spreads her legs apart and puts his penis deep inside her.

Homosexual Fellatio

A. Joe, a dark young man, is seated on the bed. He is slender, extremely good looking, and nude. Mel comes out of the shower, a towel wrapped around his waist. He looks at his partner and appreciates his lean, angular body. He lets the towel slip from his waist, the light-haired man begins to fondle his own penis. Joe watches as his strong muscular partner becomes erect. The movements of the lighter man, the strong large hand encircling the now bulging, straining penis, excite him. He begins to breathe heavily. "I can take care of that for you," Mel replies. This makes Joe even more excited. He feels and sees himself enlarge. His nerves and muscles are tightening. The lighter man comes over to the bed and sits next to his partner. His right hand remains on his own penis. He places his left hand on the dark man's right leg. They look at each other, as Mel moves his hand up and down his penis, up and down his partner's tense, taut leg. The darker man begins to grow and aches to be touched. The lighter man allows his left hand to move up the inside of his partner's leg, just barely touching the testicles. Joe squirms and opens his mouth while Mel bends down to a huge penis and begins to suck it.

B. In an elegantly furnished bedroom suite, a reddish-haired man of medium height and medium weight is lying flat on a neatly made bed with a very expensive bedspread. He wears only a jockstrap. He is thinking about his lover who is soon to arrive. When he hears a knock on the door, the man says nothing. The door opens and a tall blond man with a mustache and beard walks in. The blond man is immaculately dressed—suit, vest, tie, impeccable black shoes. The men do not speak. The blond slowly begins to undress, taking care to fold every item and place it on a nearby chair. When he is wearing only brief underwear, he walks over to the bed and bends down to kiss his partner on the mouth. The kiss lengthens. When it is over, the blond moves his body onto the bed, his head next to the other's penis. He feels his underwear pulled downward and a mouth encircle his erect penis. He opens his mouth and puts it on the penis of his partner.

C. He loves his lover's body. He fantasizes about it when they are not together. What he loves most is to use his tongue in caressing his lover's face, neck, chest, abdomen. He likes to get on his knees at the end of the bed and start kissing his lover's feet, ankles, calves. He loves squeezing the buttocks while he puts his mouth between the hairy, muscular thighs. Then he likes to pull his lover's body toward his eager, open, mouth. Grabbing the small, tight hips and letting the strained large penis enter.

Sadomasochism, Female on Male

A. Vanessa hides the ropes under the bed and places a wooden chair in the bedroom. She puts on a black garter belt and black net stockings. She wears nothing on top. Lance comes in dressed in a T-shirt and pants. When he sees Vanessa's attire he walks over to her and begins to kiss her mouth and fondle her nude breasts. He tells her that he loves to see her this way, and makes a motion to undress. Vanessa stops him and points to the chair. Lance understands that he is to sit on it. He is slightly surprised, as she has never asked him to do this before. After he sits down, Vanessa goes to the bed and brings out the ropes. His eyes glisten, and he smiles up at her. Vanessa ties his hands behind the back of the chair. He tries to catch her breasts with his mouth. Vanessa moves away and unzips his fly. Lance is becoming very excited, and feels his penis rising. He looks at her garter belt, shaping itself around her smooth white ass. Vanessa is tying his feet and firmly securing the end of the rope in a knot at the bottom of the leg of the chair. Lance is beside himself and begs her to mount him. Very slowly, Vanessa kneels down beside him and begins licking his bulging penis. Her tongue runs up and down until he yells out for her to suck it hard at the top. Lance throws back his head and moans, for her to get on top of him as she sucks.

B. A nude man is seated on a chair. He is very muscular and well built. He hears someone enter the room. It is a beautiful brunette, dressed in a lace bra and sheer underpants. She carries a brown rope. Walking over to him, she kisses him on the lips. He has dreamed of women like this, but he has never seen or been with one. He reaches out toward her, but she grabs his hands with a strength he would not have anticipated and moves them down toward the sides of the chair. She quickly moves behind the chair and winds the rope around his chest and shoulders, tying it at the back. She takes his wrists and ties them with the rope. She stands in front of him and begins to remove her bra. He is very excited, and looks down to see that he has an enormous hard-on and the tip of his penis is oozing a honeylike liquid. She slowly takes off her pants. He wants her desperately to do something to him, to take his desire and own it. She turns her back, moves toward him, straddles his legs with hers, and puts his penis inside her.

C. Dan whispers in Ellen's ear that he would like her to get out the ropes. Ellen gets up off the couch and goes to the side table, from which she removes a string of black ropes. Dan undresses while she sets a chair in the center of the room. He is smiling in anticipation. He walks toward Ellen and they kiss for a long while. Dan rubs Ellen's back and buttocks. She asks him to sit down on the chair and then binds him to it with one of the black ropes. She walks over to a desk and opens one of the drawers. Inside is a white handkerchief. She takes it over to Dan and gags him with it. Ellen opens her robe and shows Dan her curvaceous body. Dan tells her how much he wants her by looking down at his penis, which has risen majestically toward the ceiling. Slowly, she steps toward him, spreads her legs, settles herself at the top of his penis, and plunges down on him.

Male Masturbation

A. Peter is alone in his bedroom. He rises and walks toward a bookshelf. He takes out a paperback novel and begins to read about Maria and Emmanuel, dark Latin lovers who shamelessly and passionately enjoy each other. Reading about Maria's dark voluptuousness, Peter feels himself become erect. He begins to fantasize that she is in the room with him, that she wants him to do the things to her that she asks Emmanuel to do. Peter pretends that Maria is watching him as he unclasps his belt and removes his trousers. He is bulging inside his underwear. Maria is pleased and asks to see his nude penis. She takes off her blouse and shows him her heavy breasts. He gets out of his underwear and begins to manipulate his penis, all for the sake of Maria, who is thrusting her breasts toward him, asking him to enter her, pleading for him to come inside her. Peter pumps his hand up and down on his penis, asking Maria if she needs it, if she likes it, and she, beautiful and responsive, nods her head eagerly until he comes.

B. Trudy is looking directly out of her bedroom window. In the high-rise apartment next door, a nude man walks out on his balcony. He is one of the most attractive men she has ever seen. He has with him a pair of binoculars and he appears to be looking into one of the other apartments in her building. He is intent in his observation and his hand frequently falls to his left thigh, which is taut and muscular. Trudy sees that he is developing an enormous erection. Still holding the binoculars to his eyes, the man begins to grasp his penis. He rubs it hard until his body looks as if it will begin to shake. The phone rings, while Trudy watches his ejaculation.

C. Doug enjoys playing with his penis while he is with Karen. She likes to see it grow large and begin to bulge toward her. One night she asks him if he would masturbate until ejaculation in front of her. Doug thinks it might excite her and plans to stop masturbating just before he enters her. He takes her into the bedroom and he undresses. Then Doug lies flat on the bed and props his arms behind his head. "Let me watch you undress and you watch me rise." Karen begins to remove her blouse and skirt, all the while keeping her eyes on Doug's untouched growing penis. Doug becomes really excited as he watches Karen remove her bra and asks her to touch his penis. "No," she said, "you promised." Doug puts his hand on his penis and Karen begins to slowly remove her panties, taking a great deal of time and caressing herself as she does so. Doug again asks her to either touch or suck him. She remains insistent. Doug then begins to pump himself up and down as he watches Karen slither out of her panties and begin to writhe and groan as she touches her breasts, her vagina. Doug feels himself bursting as he quickly starts to rub the underside of the penis's head, then encircles the lower part and moves his hand up and down until, just as Karen is moving to get on top of him, his semen scatters all over the bed.

Homosexual Anal Intercourse

A. The blond, muscular man is on his hands and knees, trembling with anticipation. His lover is behind him, speaking to him gently, as he caresses the back of the blond's legs. He talks to the blond about how much he loves to look at his buttocks, how excited he is becoming by just watching them. The blond man can feel himself getting harder. He wants his lover's penis inside him. The lover keeps talking and stroking. When he can see that his partner is taut with excitement, his whole body tense and ready, he puts his hands on the shapely buttocks, spreads them apart and inserts his huge, wet penis inside the anus. The blond lets out a cry of joy and bites his lip, waiting for his lover to move in and out, to come.

B. Donald is lying nude on the bed, fondling himself idly. He is fantasizing about his lover, who is a large, dark man, slightly older than himself. He loves gazing into his lover's eyes, kissing him on the mouth, feeling them both becoming hard together. Just then the dark man comes into the room. He looks at Donald on the bed and smiles. As he undresses, he tells his lover how much he loves looking at his young, supple body. He loves the slender legs, the curve of the back, the swell of the buttocks. He comes to the end of the bed and asks Donald to move downward, as he lubricates his penis. When the buttocks are almost at the edge of the bed, the dark man puts his hands underneath them and raises the slender legs up into the air. He gently tips the young man so that he can see the spread of the buttocks, the opening of the anus. Bending down, he begins to kiss the hair surrounding the penis. He licks the testicles. Then, feeling himself harden, he raises himself up, still holding the legs up and back. Slowly, he inserts himself into the open anus, staring down at the spread buttocks, the trembling legs.

C. They are lying together nude on the bed, fondling each other's penises, kissing and exploring each other with their tongues. The shorter man is somewhat stocky, hairy, muscular. The taller man is lighter in hair color and complexion, slender and delicate in his looks. The stockier one is stroking the slender thighs of his partner and bends down so that he can take the long penis into his mouth. His lover moans and turns over on the bed. Quickly the stocky partner gets behind him and lifts him up so that he is on his hands and knees. Taking his own penis into his hand, the stockier man begins rubbing it until he becomes quite hard and wet. He stares at his lover's buttocks, bends to kiss both sides. Then he raises himself up, grabs his lover by the hips, and puts his penis deep inside the hot, tight anus.

Nude Male

A. Elizabeth walks into the billiards room of a large mansion where a party is being held. She is surprised to see a man, alone and completely nude, leaning against a pool table. He is extremely handsome, his face turned to one side, absorbed in some thought of his own and unaware that she has entered. The light in the room casts a long shadow down the front of the man's torso. His wide, smooth shoulders and his strong muscular arms are cast in a golden glow. Elizabeth can see the dark pubic hair and also his penis, resting lightly on the side of the table. His hands clasp the side of the pool table. He turns his eyes toward her.

B. Lynne and Robert are lying on their stomachs, stretched out on towels on the deck of a small boat. The sun is hot on their skin. Lynne looks up and sees a man swimming toward the side of the boat. As he approaches, he yells to them to throw down the portable ladder so that he can climb onto the deck. Lynne throws him the ladder and watches as he slowly climbs up. He has a beautifully strong, slender body, all golden and baked from the sun. His legs are long and muscular. There are intense little ripples in his thighs. As he raises his right leg to place it on the last rung, Lynne can see his penis, dripping with the sun-sparked, glistening driblets of water.

C. The young man is dark, his eyes deep set, his nose classically sculpted, his mouth full and sensual. He is lying stretched out nude on a rich oriental rug, his hands behind his head. His arms are strong, the muscles of the upper arm bulging in all the appropriate places. His torso is bathed in light from the open doorway. His buttocks are slightly raised off the floor, and his long white thighs are taut and tense. His penis, erect and very large, points to his right, stretched out at an angle against his upper hip. It is bulging, the veins visible, the testicles swelling beneath.

Partially Clad Male

A. Through the half-opened doorway Janice could see a man standing up, his back to her. He was of medium height and weight, and he was wearing only a pair of brief bikini shorts. He began to remove them, grasping their sides and slowly sliding them down his body. As he bent downward, the play of light and shadow allowed her to see his buttocks and legs, strong and muscular. A shaft of shadow ran down the inside of his right thigh.

B. Unaware that anyone was watching, a beautifully bronzed athletic man walked along a sun-drenched beach and removed his jacket. Underneath, his chest was bare and broad. He wore a pair of white pants and a leather belt. His face was intense, strong, and masculine. The muscles of his arms were very large, and his hands fell at the side of his body.

C. A powerfully muscular man is lying on his back on the beach. He is well tanned, and he is wearing a pair of bright blue swim trunks. Around his neck is a leather chain with a small silver ornament hanging from the center. His legs are strong, his thighs wide. He unbuttons the top of his trunks and slides the zipper down so that the cloth covers the top of his penis. At his side is a pack of cigarettes. He reaches for one, lights it, and stretches his body out comfortably on the sand.

4 The Sexual Consensus: Results

BEFORE presenting my actual study results, it seems appropriate to repeat here a statement made by Kinsey in 1953:

> While we may emphasize the differences that exist between the average male and female, it should be borne in mind that there are many individuals . . . who widely depart from these averages.[1]

When comparing your own preferences with the results of the study, please keep this point in mind. Preferences for particular sexual activities are highly individual and private. The results of the study provide us with a norm; they reveal the sexual preferences of a particular sampling of the population. There will always be individual differences that are perfectly normal and healthy. In matters of sex, the individual man or woman is the best person to determine what is exciting and fulfilling for himself or herself.

I will begin by presenting the results of female preferences for sexual activities. The mean rankings —the computed average for both male and female responses—can be found in Table C in the Appendix. In this chapter, I will discuss some of the reasons that I perceive to be behind these particular choices. For purposes of brevity and clarity, I will focus primarily on the top ten thematic preferences for each sex. This does not, of course, mean that the other nine themes are of no significance, but only that, as they represent activities that are not as sexually stimulating to the subjects as were others, they are less relevant to our purpose of determining priorities of preference based on excitatory value of the photographs.

In these discussions, I will refer to the *preferred*

activity; e.g., women rated *cunnilingus* as "their most preferred activity." I remind the reader that, for the purposes of the study, preference for sexual activity was measured by the degree of excitatory response to photographic representations of sexual *themes.* I measured reactivity to the photographic depiction of the theme and inferred from the degree of reactivity a preference for sexual theme.

WHAT SEXUAL ACTIVITIES WOMEN PREFER FOR THEMSELVES

TABLE 1
Results of Female Rankings for Photographs

Ranking Order	*Theme*
1	Heterosexual cunnilingus: oral sex, male on female
2	Triad: two males and one female joined together and engaged in coitus and/or oral-genital activity
3	Heterosexual petting, both nude
4	Heterosexual intercourse, female on top of male
5	Heterosexual petting, both partially clad
6	Heterosexual intercourse, male on top of female
7	Sadomasochism, male on female
8	Nude male
9	Heterosexual fellatio: oral sex, female on male
10	Male masturbation
11	Homosexual fellatio
12	Sadomasochism, female on male
13	Partially clad male
14	Homosexual cunnilingus
15	Nude female
16	Female masturbation
17	Homosexual petting, female
18	Partially clad female
19	Homosexual anal intercourse

1. Heterosexual Cunnilingus: Oral Sex, Male on Female

In 1953 Kinsey found oral-genital contact to be considered by the majority of his female sample as abnormal and perverse, with a very small percentage actually participating in this sexual activity.[1] The results of my study directly contradict this earlier data. Women rated cunnilingus as their most preferred activity, most likely because of the intense physiological pleasure that occurs when a soft tongue caresses the clitoris. Freud's theoretical insistence that only a vaginal orgasm could be considered a mature orgasm has been previously disproven, and the results of my study certainly confirm the fact that many mature women are opting for the pleasure of clitoral stimulation and orgasm over full vaginal penetration by the penis. Interestingly enough, however, women rarely articulate or acknowledge this preference to men. In working with women patients, I am frequently amazed to hear them express their inability to communicate their desire for cunnilingus to their partners. Often women feel guilty in asking for cunnilingus because they feel they are being "selfish" or are not attending to the needs of the male. "What's in it for him?" one of my patients recently asked me. Also, negative learning experiences in childhood and adolescence reinforce a woman's feeling that the vagina and the clitoris are "dirty" areas of their body and that a man would be repulsed or disgusted by oral contact with them. In *The Women's Room,* Marilyn French's best-selling novel, one of the characters, Mira, has her first experience with oral sex at the age of forty. Her first reaction is horror: "Then his head moved down, and she tightened up, her eyes widened, he was kissing her genitals, licking them, she was horrified. . . ."[2] The novel goes on to describe Mira's expansion of passion and pleasure as her lover attends to her clitoris: "He was rubbing her clitoris, gently, slowly, ritually, and she was making little gasps that she could hear from a distance . . ." and "Her clitoris was being triggered again, and it felt sharp and fierce and hot and as full of pain as pleasure. . . ."[3] Mira came from a middle-class background, with all its restrictions and reservations about sex, and she learned her lessons well. Obviously, however, what a woman *learns* as appropriate sexual behavior is not synonymous with the actual activities her body desires and her mind prefers.

2. Triad: Two Males and One Female Joined Together and Engaged in Coitus and/or Oral-Genital Activity

Women chose as their second most preferred sexual activity the involvement with two men in coitus and/or oral sex. This choice is interesting because most women would be surprised by its popularity and consider a woman who actually engaged in such activity as "deviant." Taking on two sexual partners at a time is definitely not what women in this society have been encouraged to do. Men often hire a number of females for their own individual and/or group pleasure, but this option has rarely been offered to women. The triad is, however, obviously pleasurable and exciting to a number of women. Whether or not they choose to indulge in this practice, the idea of being pursued by more than one male is extremely attractive to women, and may have helped to make Mary McGregor's country and western song "Torn Between Two Lovers" a popular hit. In the triad, a woman can experience herself as tremendously desirable and attractive; she has two men competing for her charms. Also, she can experience increased stimulation by the addition of another set of hands, mouth, and an extra penis. Who can fight the old adage that two heads are better than one?

3. Heterosexual Petting, Both Nude

Most men and women would probably agree that women enjoy foreplay in and of itself and not necessarily as a prelude to intercourse. Women did, in fact, choose the theme of foreplay as their third most preferred choice. Shere Hite has commented that foreplay is necessary for female sexual fulfillment "because there is so little real stimulation for women involved in intercourse."[4] This seems too narrow an interpretation because it confines the necessity of foreplay to a function of physiological need. I think that no matter how radical our changes in the relationships between men and women, women will continue to experience foreplay as an extremely important dimension of their sexual encounters. Not only do kissing and caressing help to arouse a woman's body in physical preparation for intercourse, they also provide her with the emotional and psychological assurance of care and affection from her partner.

4. Heterosexual Intercourse, Female on Top of Male

This choice provides interesting news about female sexuality because it directly challenges the culturally accepted assumption that women enjoy and gratefully accept the passive role in sex. The results of my study show that women like to take the initiative and assume some control in sexual activity. In *The Women's Room,* for example, the newly awakened Mira for the first time in her life takes responsibility and control for what happens in the sexual encounter. Mira represents a woman who acts out her desire to control the conditions of her own desire and pleasure, specifically that of performing intercourse on top of a man. Masters and Johnson's research has shown that the female superior position in intercourse offers possibilities for increased clitoral stimulation.[5] Also, as Mira's experience suggests, a woman has greater freedom for movement and varied patterns of rhythms when she is in the superior position. And there is the added visual stimulation, as the female can, in this position, better observe her own and her partner's body.

5. Heterosexual Petting, Both Partially Clad

This choice reaffirms the importance of foreplay for a woman. She wants to be sexually stimulated, and she wants it to be a slow building process. Also, the partially clad petting replays for a woman her early sexual experiences where she was asked to be "gatekeeper" or guardian of her virginity and reputation. In a mature sexual encounter, a woman can indulge herself in the "heavy petting" scenario by recalling the thrills and titillations of earlier experiences that she had to stop. She can now go beyond the early experience, but still savor the excitation of that which is forbidden.

The partially clad petting theme is attractive to women also because it nourishes their sense of romance and courtship. In a previous study of psychosexual stimulation in men and women, researchers found that women tended to choose pictures of petting scenes that revealed romantic content.[6]

6. Heterosexual Intercourse, Male on Top of Female

Conventional intercourse with the man on top of the woman, often referred to as the missionary position, was ranked as the sixth most preferred sexual activity for women. Because of convention, conditioning, and habit, men tend to assume that this is the position women most prefer. Also, women often pretend to their partners that they enjoy this position above all others, even, in fact, fake orgasms to confirm their pleasure. Men obviously take this as actual preference and pleasure in women and, therefore, continue to practice this form of intercourse to the exclusion of other forms and other activities. If a couple engages in the missionary position alone, it is highly unlikely that experimentation and variety will occur. Yet women reveal in their rankings the desire and need for other sexual activities and practices. It is interesting, for example, that women find nude petting scenes more stimulating than scenes of intercourse with a woman on top, and partially clad petting scenes more stimulating than scenes of intercourse in the missionary position.

7. *Sadomasochism, Male on Female*

Women reveal in this choice what seems to be a desire often referred to as the "rape fantasy." It exists within every woman who has ever dreamed about being overpowered and overwhelmed by an attractive, sexually aggressive male. This does not mean that such women go out on the street at night panting for the possibility of a rape. Rape in a dark alley by a violent stranger is a traumatic and harmful experience. Policemen and prosecutors are aware of the rape fantasy in women, and they often misinterpret the fantasy as a real desire to be raped. No woman would choose the terror, horror, danger, and brutalization of an actual rape to fulfill this fantasy. In the selected corners of her own mind, a woman can fantasize a rape in which her partner is as gentle, attractive, and stimulating as she likes. The rape fantasy allows for the possibility of the choice of partner and conditions. Many of my patients reveal in their fantasies and dreams the desire to be overtaken sexually by a man who is attractive to them. It is not only highly stimulating to fantasize this particular sexual situation; it also removes from the female any sense of responsibility in making the choice to have sex and, therefore, eliminates any guilt she may have about indulging in sexual behavior. If a woman has been brought up to believe that having sex is "naughty" and "wrong," something that "nice" girls don't do, then the rape fantasy allows her to indulge her sexual yearnings and desires without feeling that she has initiated or requested the sexual act. Tied up and gagged, she can only gesture a "Look, Ma, no hands." The message is, of course, "I'm enjoying this, but it's not my fault."

8. *Nude Male*

This choice reflects a healthy and increasing source of stimulation that women are now experiencing, the freedom to express their appreciation for the nude male body. When Kinsey was collecting his data on female sexual attitudes, he found that women most frequently reported feelings of repugnance and distaste at the sight of the male body, particularly at the sight of an erection.[7] It has only been recently that women have had opportunities for viewing male anatomy (even unerect) in magazines such as *Playgirl* and at clubs. Until now, the only place a female could publicly view a male was in an art museum, where she could disguise an erotic interest with aesthetic concern. Now, however, photos of nude males are being designed for females, and women are showing their interest and appreciation. The inhibiting influences of the culture have kept women from acknowledging their natural attraction to the male body. To a healthy, responsive woman, the sight of an erect penis can be a powerful erotic stimulant.

9. Heterosexual Fellatio: Oral Sex, Female on Male

One of the most important pleasures that a woman derives from fellatio is that it is so totally pleasing to the male. Women learn that providing pleasure for a man is one of her primary functions. They know that fellatio gives a man extreme pleasure, and they feel that if they can grant such pleasure, they are then accredited sexual creatures. Therapist Carmen Kerr comments that, in the traditional view, "Good sex is when he enjoys it and when she's glad he does."[8] In performing fellatio, however, a woman can actually derive pleasure from giving this experience to a man. Mira, Marilyn French's late-to-bloom heroine, forbade the practice of fellatio in the strict confines of her lifeless, loveless marriage. In a vital sexual relationship with her new lover, Mira takes delight and pleasure in performing fellatio. The very act of providing intense pleasure to the male becomes itself a source of sexual stimulation to the female. Also, physiologically, the penis rubbing inside the mouth provides a stimulation for the mucous membranes, very similar to that which occurs in a French kiss. Performing fellatio also fulfills the primal instinct for sucking, which, in our contemporary society of overweight smokers, is an obvious fixation.

10. Male Masturbation

This choice reaffirms woman's interest in the male nude body and, also, her attraction for and appreciation of an erect penis. If a male is masturbating, he is intently focused on the sexual interest, his penis is erect, and he is expressing sexual concentration and virility. Again, the erect penis can be a source of erotic stimulation for women.

It is interesting that the eleventh choice for women was *homosexual fellatio,* ranking only two points lower than *heterosexual fellatio.* Women do find homosexual themes somewhat sexually stimulating and, in general, tend to be more stimulated by homosexuality in the opposite sex than homosexuality in their own sex. This was not the case, however, in the ranking of *homosexual anal intercourse.* Women and, we will see when we look at the male data, men as well, found this to be the least sexually stimulating theme.

Also interesting is the fact that women ranked *sadomasochism, female on male,* a relatively high twelfth. This is surprising in light of social encouragement for women to adopt the passive role. In this sexual theme, women are represented as being in total control and the truly aggressive and dominant partner. Women apparently find it somewhat sexually stimulating to behave in ways directly opposite to those to which they have been conditioned.

Women also ranked the *nude female* relatively high (fifteenth). Freudian theory would explain this female interest in the female body as a form of latent homosexuality that exists in all women because their first love object is a female, namely her mother. I think that the reason women find a nude female to be somewhat sexually stimulating is that this particular theme has, through "girlie" magazines and nude calendar photos, come to represent sex in the minds of both men and women. Women have a conditioned reflex to seeing a nude female photograph, and immediately associate it with heterosexual activity.

In looking at the results of male preference for sexual activity, it is important to remember that the males who participated in this study were in the same age range as the females, and, therefore, we can assume they shared with the females comparable levels of sexual experience and maturity. Once again, be prepared for some surprises.

Male preferences for sexual activity as determined by this study surprisingly contradict the assumptions about men that are perpetrated by the current *macho* philosophy. For example, contrary to the general consensus that men prefer intercourse above all other forms of sexual exploration and activity, males in this study rated heterosexual coitus in the missionary position as their ninth choice. Their first preference, like the females, was for oral sex, with the opposite sex in the active role.

WHAT SEXUAL ACTIVITIES MEN PREFER FOR THEMSELVES

TABLE 2

Results of Male Rankings of Photographs

Ranking Order	*Theme*
1	Heterosexual fellatio: oral sex, female on male
2	Nude female
3	Heterosexual intercourse, female on top of male
4	Heterosexual petting, both nude
5	Partially clad female
6	Triad: two males and one female joined together and engaged in coitus and/or oral-genital activity
7	Sadomasochism, female on male
8	Heterosexual cunnilingus: oral sex, male on female
9	Heterosexual intercourse, male on top of female
10	Heterosexual petting, partially clad

TABLE 2 (*continued*)

Ranking Order	*Theme*
11	Sadomasochism, male on female
12	Homosexual cunnilingus
13	Female masturbation
14	Homosexual petting, female
15	Homosexual fellatio
16	Partially clad male
17	Male masturbation
18	Nude male
19	Homosexual anal intercourse

1. Heterosexual Fellatio: Oral Sex, Female on Male

It is the consensus of the sexes that oral sex rates number one. Both men and women acknowledge that oral sex, with the opposite sex in the active role, is their most preferred sexual activity. There are a number of possible reasons for the male preference for fellatio. Women through the ages have served as tools or rewards for men, and having a woman perform fellatio is one way for a man to confirm her as an accessory to his own pleasure and need. More important, however, this experience allows a male to abandon his culturally defined role as aggressor in the "missionary" position of sexual intercourse and take on the role of recipient. In enjoying fellatio, a man need not be at work as he is in other activities where he attempts to stimulate and please his partner. His entire body can be restful, and he is not asked to return anything or worry about the responses of his partner. Although he has the opportunity to put his hands on his partner's head and in that way regulate the depth and speed of her activity, the experience of fellatio is, for the man, completely self-pleasing and self-oriented. Also, and this is most likely true for women too, oral sex with the opposite sex in the active role provides some gratifying visual stimulation for the recipient.

2. Nude Female

Men selected photographs of nude females as their second most favored theme. Since there is no specific sexual activity expressed in these photographs, it may be assumed that the theme elicits a conditioned response from males. Pornographic pictures of nude females are a part of a male's curriculum in the course of his developing sexuality. It is the rare male who completes adolescence without the experience of masturbating over a photograph of a nude female body. One of the advantages of this experience for both adolescent and adult males is that it allows even those who feel insecure about their attractiveness to women to have feelings of sexual prowess and success with a "woman" of their own choice.

3. Heterosexual Intercourse: Female on Top of Male

Both men and women prefer intercourse with the woman on top over the conventional position. This preference in males challenges the cultural conception that men consistently favor being in the dominant, active role. As with a woman, what a man learns is his socially determined responsibility, if not necessarily what he wants and prefers. As in fellatio, the male enjoys being "acted upon" when his partner is on top of him. He can release himself from the responsibility of manipulation and penetration and can give himself over to the pleasure of his partner's motions. He can also be increasingly stimulated by viewing the body and activity of his partner, and can indulge with the freedom of his hands in caressing her breasts and buttocks.

4. Heterosexual Petting, Both Nude

This choice reveals a significant piece of good news for both sexes. It has previously been assumed that males merely "endure" the period of foreplay for the sake of the female. This self-reported preference indicates that men find foreplay an important and pleasurable part of the sexual experience and value it almost as highly as women do. As the sexual behavior of both sexes is determined by their earlier upbringing, it would appear that the adolescent activity of heavy petting carries over into adulthood. The very experiences that adolescents have in their initial approaches to sexuality—lying close, kissing, touching, running their hands over each other's body—are apparently very important in adult sexuality.

5. Partially Clad Female

This theme, like the nude female, affords an opportunity for male fantasy. In the mind of the male, the subject can become as pliable and cooperative as he chooses, and she presents no real threat or demand for sexual activity or her own pleasure. As with women, a situation where one or both partners are partially clothed stimulates a sense of romance as well as the challenge of the "chase." The female is there for the male to undress at his pace and his choosing. She can, in other words, be "conquered" through the act of undressing. What adolescent boy has not experienced a sense of conquest when he first manages to unsnap a bra? Each article of clothing that is removed heightens the feeling of excitement, anticipation, and power.

6. Triad: Two Males and One Female Joined Together and Engaged in Coitus and/or Oral-Genital Activity

Common sense dictates that if my male subjects had had their choice, they would have preferred to view pictures on this theme with two females and one male. This variation was not, however, included in the study. It is somewhat surprising to learn that males find sharing a woman so highly stimulating. Men often report, however, that it is extremely stimulating to see a female in a state of sexual excitement, even if they themselves are not the agents of arousal. This probably accounts for the tremendous amount of pornographic material devoted to the theme of female homosexuality. Although in this study, men ranked *homosexual cunnilingus* and *homosexual petting, female,* relatively low (twelfth and fourteenth respectively), there is ample evidence that men find it stimulating to observe situations where two women are exciting each other or where another man is involved in the stimulation of a female.[9] In these instances, many of the fears and concerns that a man has about his sexuality are removed. He doesn't have to worry about failing, premature ejaculation, inadequate performance, or anything else. The female is being "prepared" for him, and he is released of some of the responsibility for getting her ready. While conventional attitudes may confirm the concepts of monogamy, sexual possession, and male superiority, the selection of the triad suggests that males, at least in their fantasies, are willing to share a female, work together in granting her pleasure, and consider her desires and preferences as top priorities. Men also may find it appealing to have the opportunity to have sexual relations in the company of another man in a comparatively socially sanctioned setting. That is, most men would prefer to admit that they learned about another male's sexuality in the company of a female than alone with another male. This may satisfy male curiosity about other males' sexual behavior with both a man and a woman. Men are also highly competitive and may relish the idea of discovering what forms their competition takes and also the possibility of "outdoing" one another by providing increased stimulation for the female.

7. Sadomasochism, Female on Male

Once again, in affirming a preference for passivity, men are confirming a need and desire to be released from the expected patterns of assertion, aggression, control, and activity that the culture has placed upon them. The physical restraints in this theme allow the male the freedom *not to do.* The woman, in tying and gagging the man, is giving him license to enjoy the experience while she takes full responsibility for sexual manipulation and contact. In *Men in Love,* a study of male sexual fantasy, Nancy Friday observes that men express, over and over again, a desire for domination by an authoritarian female. One of Friday's major contentions is that men want to feel that women like sex, that they will say yes to sex, that they will affirm sexual pleasure and contact.[10] When a woman takes the aggressive role and overpowers a man in the sexual encounter, she is filling the male need for female affirmation of sex.

8. Heterosexual Cunnilingus: Oral Sex, Male on Female

As women can derive sexual pleasure and satisfaction from giving men the pleasures of fellatio, men experience satisfaction from pleasing a woman through cunnilingus. Also, by watching a woman's response to cunnilingus, a man can become highly stimulated.

He is being a sexual creature by granting intense pleasure to his partner. Contrary to some of the statements made by recent commentators on male sexuality, the male preference for cunnilingus reveals that men are not villains, exclusively concerned with their own needs and satisfactions. Rather, they are extremely interested in providing their partners with intense pleasure and satisfaction.

9. Heterosexual Intercourse: Male on Top of Female

The popular opinion held on male sexuality is that men would choose conventional intercourse over other forms of sexual behavior. In reality, however, men find this less sexually interesting than a variety of other activities. This is not to say, of course, that men don't desire intercourse; but they do find other activities more exciting and stimulating. Also, if they do choose intercourse men prefer to have their female partners in the dominant position.

10. Heterosexual Petting, Both Partially Clad

This choice reaffirms the male interest in participating and sharing in the sexual experience rather than simply dominating it. Again, men are not merely after orgasmic responses, but also like to express care and affection to their partners.

The eleventh choice for men was *sadomasochism, male on female.* This shows us that while men reveal preferences for themes that place them in passive roles, they also like, at times, to have total control and dominance in manipulating and stimulating their partners. Apparently, both men and women have the capacity to act out and enjoy both the passive and the aggressive roles in sexual situations.

The male preferences followed the model of the

female preferences in that neither sex chose a homosexual theme as one of the top ten preferences. Also, men, like women, revealed that they preferred homosexual themes involving the opposite sex. Men ranked *homosexual cunnilingus* twelfth and *homosexual petting, female,* fourteenth. This indicates that there is some heterosexual interest in viewing homosexual themes. Both males and females found it more stimulating to view members of the opposite sex involved in homosexual activities.

The single exception to this was the ranking of *homosexual anal intercourse.* One of the findings of the study was that both men and women agreed that this theme was the least sexually stimulating. It is possible that the strong social condemnation that accompanies this theme is partially responsible for its very low ranking.

The results of female and male preferences for sexual activities reveal some rather dramatic similarities and differences. Both sexes, for example, prefer oral sex performed on them by the opposite sex as their favorite activity. The similarity, however, is the difference—for in this case men rank *fellatio* first and *cunnilingus* eighth while women chose *cunnilingus* first and *fellatio* ninth. Both men and women enjoy foreplay, women preferring foreplay before intercourse, men preferring intercourse above petting. Perhaps one of the most important similarities is that both men and women chose intercourse with the female in the superior position as preferable to intercourse in the traditional or "missionary" position.

The results also reveal that both sexes often prefer sexual activities that are contradictory to the social and cultural expectations. For example, given the early sex training of men and women, we might expect men to prefer *macho* activities where they are constantly in control, and women to prefer more passive activities and ones that do not involve oral-genital contact. Obviously, this is not the case.

I think it is fair to say that the majority of men and women develop their sexual behavior patterns as a result of the sex education and training they experience in early life. The results of my study show that often men and women would prefer to indulge in radically different activities but it is a fairly safe assumption that generally they are performing conventional sexual activities based on assumed behavioral patterns which cannot really satisfy them.

The similarities, differences, and contradictions that attend the sexual preferences of males and females are extremely important. Throughout the remainder of the book we will attempt to determine their significance and relevance to ourselves as adults in contemporary life and also their relevance to the sex education of our children. In order to make this more personally meaningful, I now invite the reader to compare your own results from the self-test with the results of the study.

AN OVERVIEW OF THE RESULTS

INSTRUCTIONS:

This chart enables you to see the results of all parts of the study. The blank sections provide you with space to fill in your own results obtained from the self-test in Chapter Three.

MY SEXUAL PREFERENCES

Themes

Heterosexual intercourse, male on top of female	______
Heterosexual intercourse, female on top of male	______
Heterosexual petting, both nude	______
Heterosexual petting, both partially clad	______
Heterosexual fellatio: oral sex, female on male	______
Nude female	______
Heterosexual cunnilingus: oral sex, male on female	______
Female masturbation	______
Triad: two males and one female joined together and engaged in coitus and/or oral-genital activity	______
Partially clad female	______
Homosexual cunnilingus	______
Homosexual petting, female	______
Sadomasochism, male on female	______
Homosexual fellatio	______
Sadomasochism, female on male	______
Male masturbation	______
Homosexual anal intercourse	______
Nude male	______
Partially clad male	______

FEMALE SEXUAL PREFERENCES

Ranking Order	*Theme*
1	Heterosexual cunnilingus: oral sex, male on female
2	Triad: two males and one female joined together and engaged in coitus and/or oral-genital activity
3	Heterosexual petting, both nude
4	Heterosexual intercourse, female on top of male
5	Heterosexual petting, both partially clad

Ranking Order	Theme
6	Heterosexual intercourse, male on top of female
7	Sadomasochism, male on female
8	Nude male
9	Heterosexual fellatio: oral sex, female on male
10	Male masturbation
11	Homosexual fellatio
12	Sadomasochism, female on male
13	Partially clad male
14	Homosexual cunnilingus
15	Nude female
16	Female masturbation
17	Homosexual petting, female
18	Partially clad female
19	Homosexual anal intercourse

MALE SEXUAL PREFERENCES

Ranking Order	Theme
1	Heterosexual fellatio: oral sex, female on male
2	Nude female
3	Heterosexual intercourse, female on top of male
4	Heterosexual petting, both nude
5	Partially clad female
6	Triad: two males and one female joined together and engaged in coitus and/or oral-genital activity
7	Sadomasochism, female on male
8	Heterosexual cunnilingus: oral sex, male on female
9	Heterosexual intercourse, male on top of female
10	Heterosexual petting, partially clad
11	Sadomasochism, male on female
12	Homosexual cunnilingus
13	Female masturbation
14	Homosexual petting, female

Ranking Order	*Theme*
15	Homosexual fellatio
16	Partially clad male
17	Male masturbation
18	Nude male
19	Homosexual anal intercourse

In the next chapter, we will take a look at the ways in which men and women predict or fail to predict accurately what they believe to be sexually stimulating to their own and the opposite sex. This information can help in getting rid of a number of distortions in thinking that prevent the sexes from understanding themselves and each other.

5 Sexual Speculations: How Men and Women Perceive Preferences of the Opposite Sex

WE all have preconceived notions about what other men and women prefer sexually. When confronted with the task of actually assigning priorities to those activities, we may find ourselves wondering just where our opinions came from. This can be a puzzling experience.

As we review the results of this next portion of my study—how men and women perceive one another's preferences—I will explore some of the dynamics behind the assumptions that made the subjects respond as they did. We should keep in mind that obviously none of the subjects had any prior knowledge of my findings since the findings had not yet been determined. Both men and women were merely conjecturing, on an individual basis, what they thought other men and women would prefer.

To the best of my knowledge at the time of this writing, no data are available on the ability of males and females to predict one another's sexual preferences nor on their ability to predict preferences within their own sex.

In this chapter I will present all predictions of the opposite sex: male estimates of female preferences, and female estimates of male preferences. In the next chapter, I will present predictions of the same sex: female estimates of female preferences, and male estimates of male preferences. I will not cover every individual theme, but will discuss only those that appear to be most meaningful and educational. On some themes I will comment briefly; on others I will go into considerable detail.

THE MALE VIEW OF FEMALE SEXUALITY

TABLE 3
Male Estimates of Female Preferences for Sexual Activity

Theme	*True Female Rank*	*Male Estimated Rank for Females*
Heterosexual cunnilingus: oral sex, male on female	1	3
Triad: two males and one female joined together and engaged in coitus and/or oral-genital activity	2	7
Heterosexual petting, both nude	3	4
Heterosexual intercourse, female on top of male	4	2
Heterosexual petting, both partially clad	5	5
Heterosexual intercourse, male on top of female	6	1
Sadomasochism, male on female	7	12
Nude male	8	8
Heterosexual fellatio: oral sex, female on male	9	6
Male masturbation	10	11
Homosexual fellatio	11	16
Sadomasochism, female on male	12	9
Partially clad male	13	10
Homosexual cunnilingus	14	14

TABLE 3 (*continued*)

Theme	*True Female Rank*	*Male Estimated Rank for Females*
Nude female	15	18
Female masturbation	16	15
Homosexual petting, female	17	13
Partially clad female	18	17
Homosexual anal intercourse	19	19

WHAT THE RESULTS MEAN

Heterosexual Cunnilingus, Oral Sex, Male on Female

Women ranked cunnilingus number 1 as their most preferred sexual activity. Men estimated it for women as number 3. While they were fairly accurate in predicting that *cunnilingus* is highly stimulating to women, most men express a great deal of surprise that this is actually the number one sexual preference for females. An interesting exception to this is television host Tom Snyder, who, when I appeared as a guest on his late-night show, made this comment: "Show me a man who does not like cunnilingus, and I'll steal his girl."

Triad: Two Males and One Female Joined Together and Engaged in Coitus and/or Oral-Genital Activity

Women ranked the triad as number 2 in their sexual preferences. Men estimated it for women as number 7, underestimating its highly stimulating value for females. The male inability to perceive that women would become excited over the idea of performing oral-genital activity with two lovers reveals, I think, a fundamental misconception that men, and, in fact, some women, hold about women. There is an unspoken expectation that women would be more stimulated by conventional and socially acceptable sexual activities and also that women would not be stimulated by the more deviant or "abnormal" sexual practices. It would appear that it is more socially acceptable for a man to be involved with more than one woman, and that males would therefore be more stimulated by the idea of that type of triad. There is also perhaps the possibility that a man would feel fear or jealousy and see his role as a male threatened if a woman stated a preference for two lovers rather than one. Both the structure of the male ego and the society find comfort in believing that women prefer monogamy.

The Foreplay Themes: Heterosexual Petting, Both Nude, and Heterosexual Petting, Both Partially Clad

Women ranked *heterosexual petting, nude,* as number 3 and *heterosexual petting, partially clad,* as number 5 in their sexual preferences. Men estimated these for women at numbers 4 and 5 respectively. The accuracy with which males predicted sexual preference for both petting themes supports the view that men tend to perceive women as enjoying traditional forms of sexual activity. They also may be recalling female behavior and preference in adolescence, when petting is the primary focus and sometimes the pinnacle of sexual involvement. I have frequently heard women complain about the absence of foreplay in their lovemaking. They miss the excitement of anticipation and the gradual progression toward intercourse. It is quite possible that females express to men this nostalgic claim, feeling more comfortable in admitting an interest in an activity that is not directly intercourse-oriented. For women, intercourse per se is represented in their youth as the ultimate sin. Petting, by contrast, is a rather mild and fairly acceptable indulgence. Therefore, it seems, women feel safer and more comfortable in expressing this preference to men.

Heterosexual Intercourse, Female on Top of Male

Women ranked this activity as number 4 in their sexual preferences. Men estimated it for women as number 2. From their predictions of female preferences, it appears that men perceive that women prefer heterosexual intercourse above all other sexual alternative activities presented in the study. Men assumed that women would choose *heterosexual intercourse, male on top of female,* as their most preferred sexual activity and, when asked what a woman's next choice would be, they assumed that a woman would naturally choose another form of *intercourse, female on top of male*—rather than a sexual activity of a less conventional nature. I believe this male prediction confirms the fact that most men tend to perceive women as appreciating and enjoying sexual activities that are regarded as conventional, socially desirable, and acceptable.

Heterosexual Intercourse, Male on Top of Female

Women ranked this activity as number 6. Men estimated it for women, interestingly, as number 1. This is a very significant discrepancy in the males' ability to predict the relative excitatory value of the most commonly practiced form of sexual activity for women.[1] Men are saying here that they believe that women enjoy the most conventional form of sexual activity and that they enjoy male dominance in intercourse more than anything else. With the exception of *sadomasochism, male on female,* this is the theme that reveals the male in the most aggressive position and in the position of greatest control. This one piece of information evidences the distortions of thinking that so often occur in anticipating sexual preferences. One of the reasons for this particular distortion is that women, thinking that men *want* them to like this conventional activity, often fake their responses in an attempt to convince men that they actually do. Women must believe that it is important for a man to feel in control and, literally, "on top" of the situation. In trying to protect a man's feelings, a woman will often lie about how much she enjoys this traditional form of sexual activity, thus encouraging the man to continue to act upon this fundamentally false assumption. It is unfortunate but true that missionary sex is the *laziest* form of intercourse, requiring least effort for the female. Men may be thinking that women, given all their negative conditioning about sexuality, may prefer to "opt out" by simply being acted upon by the male.

Sadomasochism, Male on Female

Women ranked this activity as number 7. Men estimated it for women at a lower number, 12. Although men have been aware of the rape fantasy and its appeal to women, they are apparently unaware of precisely how stimulating it is for a woman to be restrained and to feel in total possession by a male. Perhaps, as we've said, one of the reasons that this theme is so appealing to women is that it allows them to abandon responsibility for their own sexual pleasure. In adult life, we rarely have the option of being out of control. In the sexual drama, however, there is always this possibility. In the novel *9½ Weeks,* a female executive records a period of her life where by day she lived a responsible adult life, and at night allowed her lover to take over her entire existence.[2]

He not only bathed, fed, and clothed her; he also tied her up and exposed her to an alarming series of sexual brutalities. The interesting point about the novel is the fascination and addiction that this woman develops as she becomes increasingly dependent upon her lover's directions and demands. I think it is appealing to both men and women to have the other sex take entire control and responsibility for the sexual encounter. It is particularly appealing to women, as dramatically demonstrated in *9½ Weeks*, because of early training that suggests that sex is something that should not occur and, if it does, is the woman's fault. If a man ties a woman down and assumes complete responsibility and control, she can hardly be held accountable for what happens. Most men are not aware of this need for a woman to relieve her feelings of guilt over sex through this abandonment of responsibility. Men therefore find it difficult to believe that women would find being tied down and overwhelmed highly exciting, yet the results of the study show that restraint during the sexual activity is very pleasurable and relieving to many women.

Nude Male

Women ranked the nude male as number 8 in their sexual preferences. Men estimated it for women at exactly the same level, number 8. Males were exactly accurate in predicting how stimulating their own bodies were to women. It is interesting that they apparently know that the nude male body is to some degree sexually stimulating to women, though nowhere near as stimulating as a nude female body is to a man. Women have obviously come a long way since 1953, when Kinsey found that women described the male body as "disgusting" and "repulsive."[3] Once again, it is obvious that the media has a great deal of power in clarifying issues (as well as distorting them) for men and women. The famous Burt Reynolds center fold that appeared in *Cosmopolitan* magazine in the early 1970s was the first of its kind. It stimulated a lot of conversation that allowed both men and women to better understand and appreciate the genuine female response to the nude male body.

Heterosexual Fellatio: Oral Sex, Female on Male

Women ranked *heterosexual fellatio* as number 9. Men estimated it for women at number 6. Men seem to believe that women find fellatio more stimulating than they actually do. This may be because women are, in general, usually attempting to please a male in sexual activity rather than express and act out their own desires and preferences. In their own estimates of male sexual preferences, women predicted that men would prefer fellatio above all other sexual activities.

Male Masturbation

Women ranked *male masturbation* as number 10 in their sexual preferences. Men estimated it for women at number 11. If males are able to predict within one point that a male masturbating would be within the top ten female preferences, then perhaps with some communication between the sexes, men might begin to feel more comfortable masturbating in front of their partners, or in having their partners manually manipulate them. At times, because of a woman's menstrual period, a vaginal infection, female surgery, shaky pregnancy, or other female problems, the couple is unable to perform intercourse. Since men do not experience these sexual/physiological handicaps as frequently as women, and since they are usually physically capable of having intercourse daily, it would appear to be advantageous to work upon this knowledge that women are, if not highly, at least somewhat stimulated by male masturbation. A man could then feel comfortable, during those times when his female partner is incapacitated, in asking for her participation in his masturbatory experience.

Homosexual Fellatio

Women ranked this sexual activity as number 11. Men estimated it for women at number 16. Men are obviously unaware that male homosexuality, at least as expressed in the activity of fellatio, can be somewhat sexually stimulating to a woman. It is quite likely that men find this difficult to believe because they themselves have been taught to consider male homosexuality as repugnant and unnatural. Females, however, do not share this extremely negative view of male lovers and, while women find other aspects of male homosexuality less than desirable, this specific theme of oral sex within the male homosexual context ranks with women only one point below *male masturbation.*

I would like to comment briefly on some of the remaining eight themes. In general, men tended to believe that women would find the female homosexual themes more sexually stimulating than they actually did, although men were exactly accurate in predicting that women would rank *homosexual cunnilingus* fourteenth.

They were also exactly accurate, as was almost everybody, in predicting that *homosexual anal intercourse* would rank last. As we have seen, this is the only theme that men and women agreed on unanimously, in the preference portion of the study. Men were only one point away from accurately predicting the stimulation value of *female masturbation* and *partially clad female,* ranking them both relatively low.

Men were not so accurate in estimating how females

would rank *sadomasochism, female on male.* Men assumed that women would find this theme within the top ten of their sexual preferences, and it actually ranked twelfth. They also thought that women would rank the *partially clad male* among the top ten, when women ranked it thirteenth. The male assumption that women would more readily respond to this theme may be based on the cultural emphasis placed upon a muscular male in a bathing suit as an attractive focus for female sexual interest.

THE FEMALE VIEW OF MALE SEXUALITY

TABLE 4
Female Estimates of Male Preferences for Sexual Activity

Theme	*True Male Rank*	*Female Estimated Rank for Males*
Heterosexual fellatio: oral sex, female on male	1	1
Nude female	2	3
Heterosexual intercourse, female on top of male	3	9
Heterosexual petting, both nude	4	4
Partially clad female	5	6
Triad: two males and one female joined together and engaged in coitus and/or oral-genital activity	6	8
Sadomasochism, female on male	7	17

TABLE 4 (*continued*)

Theme	*True Male Rank*	*Female Estimated Rank for Males*
Heterosexual cunnilingus: oral sex, male on female	8	2
Heterosexual intercourse, male on top of female	9	10
Heterosexual petting, both partially clad	10	7
Sadomasochism, male on female	11	16
Homosexual cunnilingus	12	12
Female masturbation	13	5
Homosexual petting, female	14	11
Homosexual fellatio	15	13
Partially clad female	16	18
Male masturbation	17	14
Nude male	18	19
Homosexual anal intercourse	19	15

WHAT THE RESULTS MEAN

Heterosexual Fellatio: Oral Sex, Female on Male

Men ranked *heterosexual fellatio* number 1 as their most preferred sexual activity. Women correctly estimated that men would put it at number 1. Females were totally accurate in this; apparently they do know what is the most stimulating activity for men.

Although women themselves ranked this activity as ninth, they are aware that men would prefer this sexual activity above all others. We have said in an earlier chapter that men are reticent in communicating some of their sexual needs and desires. They sometimes fear that their female partners would think they are perverted if they asked, for example, to tie their partners up, or to be tied up themselves. With *fellatio*, however, the situation seems quite clear. Here a man is not asking to tie or not to tie, nor is he asking his partner to get on top of him in intercourse. He is asking her to participate in the pleasures of his own penis. He is pleased with his organ and he wants to increase his pleasure by having a woman place it in her mouth. Men apparently find it easier to ask women to perform this task, where they may have difficulty in asking them to do some of the other, less conventional, activities. Women do not appear to enjoy *fellatio* as much as some of the other sexual activties defined in the study, but they apparently understand how much men like it and are, in general, willing to perform the act.

Nude Female

Men ranked the nude female as number 2 in their sexual preferences. Women estimated it for men at a close number 3. As we will see in our discussion of male estimates of male sexual preferences, men have no idea how exciting this theme is to other men, even though they themselves find it second only to *fellatio*. Women, however, were quite accurate in predicting this theme as a high priority for male sexual stimulation. Women would seem to be more aware of the power of conditioning that photographs and the reality of a nude woman have on males. You have only to walk by any newsstand in the country to see that pictures of nude women sell. Also, women know from experience that men like to take off a woman's clothes and look at her nude body. "Take your clothes off," or, "Let me see you nude," are male directives that almost every woman has heard. The very fact that men are more stimulated by a single female rather than a heterosexual couple engaged in some sexual activity is highly interesting, but pretty obvious, in itself.

Heterosexual Intercourse, Female on Top of Male

Men ranked this sexual activity as number 3. Women estimated it for men at a somewhat lower number 9. Females failed to predict male response to this theme by as much as six points below what it actually was. Women believe, erroneously, that men prefer the much more conventional and male-dominant form of sexual intercourse. Women may also feel that men may resent a female's domination of the sexual act. The general expectation that women hold for men is that he wants to be the one in control, the one who is both figuratively and literally "on top." Women tend to assume that a man's comfort lies in being on top of the female when engaged in intercourse, and that he would feel discomfort at the passive role in intercourse. This is obviously not true. Men show that they prefer having the woman on top in intercourse to being on top of the woman, not just slightly, but by a significant six points. It is ironic that women ranked the female superior position as most highly erotic for themselves, but failed to perceive that men would share their point of view.

Heterosexual Petting, Both Nude

Men ranked this activity as number 4, and women estimated it for men at the same level. Females were exactly accurate in predicting the excitatory value of nude petting for males. I think it is safe to assume that most people have participated in this activity and do not have to rely on fantasy or conjecture to make valid predictions about it. Women apparently know that this is not the *most* stimulating activity for men and that men do have other priorities, but they also know that petting nude comes close. Certainly this is one of the most "normal" and conventional of sexual activities, and women can safely assume that men feel comfortable in engaging in it.

Partially Clad Female

Men ranked the partially clad female as number 5 in their sexual preferences. Women estimated it for men at a close number 6. As in the theme of the nude female, women were able to predict with great accuracy the excitatory value of the partially clad female, and for many of the same reasons. This then relates to all the "girlie" pictures that men have for so long been enamored of, and, apparently, women have been quite sensitive to this phenomenon.

Triad: Two Males and One Female Joined Together and Engaged in Coitus and/or Oral-Genital Activity

Men ranked the *triad* as number 6. Women estimated it for men at number 8. Females understood that this theme would rank as one of the top ten preferences for male sexual activity. If women had been totally duped by the societal assumption of the *macho* male—the champion in constant control of the sexual situation, the prizewinner in knowledge of the female anatomy and how to arouse women to sexual heights—this prediction would have turned out differently. Women were, however, quite close in accurately predicting the erotic value of the *triad* for men. Somehow, and it is probably from first-hand experience with men, women know that men may feel the need for some help in bringing the female body to the point of passionate ecstasy. Also, women are quite familiar with male competition, their need for and love of it. The *triad* can be seen as a sexual arena where men compete with each other in the attempt to give the most pleasure to the woman. Competition between males also fosters curiosity about other men's sexuality, and the *triad* is a relatively safe and unthreatening way to check this out. That women predicted within two points where men would rank the *triad*, seems to indicate that they understand on some level the feelings of inadequacy, hesitancy, and competition that men feel in the sexual situation. If a man can fantasize the help of another man in arousing a female, he has an opportunity to "size up" his competition and also to be relieved of the entire burden of sexually arousing the female.

Sadomasochism, Female on Male

Men ranked this activity as number 7 in their sexual preferences. Women estimated it for men at a very low number 17. While women were 90 percent accurate in predicting most male preferences, their inaccuracy in predicting the credit value of sadomasochism, female on male, is dramatic. This theme was depicted in the photographs by a man tied down to a chair with a female acting upon him sexually, stroking and fondling him while he was bound. The man in each picture reveals a strong erection, which suggests that he is in a state of sexual excitation. Women, however, interpreted this theme as being very low on the scale of male preference. I believe that women were so totally unprepared to accurately predict male preference for this theme because it so totally denies everything they have been taught to believe about men. Women simply assume that men would experience being tied down and restrained as a direct attack on their male ego and their need for control and aggression, supposed animalistic instincts in males. The results of male rankings of the themes of *sadomasochism, female on male, fellatio, nude female,* and *heterosexual intercourse, female on top of male,* give us very strong signals that men do at times definitely enjoy being the passive partner and allowing the female to take over and minister to the male. Removing the burden of constantly initiating and directing sexual activities seems not only to be a relief to men, but also a notion they find quite sexually stimulating as well.

Heterosexual Cunnilingus: Oral Sex, Male on Female

Men rated this activity as number 8. Women estimated it for men at a high number 2. This female prediction is rather surprising. Women apparently believe—or want to believe—that men find *cunnilingus* to be much more sexually stimulating than they actually do. There were only three other themes where women were more than six or eight points off when determining what men prefer sexually. This particular discrepancy is more surprising than any of the others because of women's general tendency to regard their own genitals as dirty or disgusting and unpleasant for male exploration. We would assume, therefore, that women would expect men to avoid choosing *cunnilingus* as a preferred sexual activity. In actuality, men are not as stimulated by this theme as women would like to believe, having chosen it as only their eighth preference. However, men did rank *cunnilingus* above intercourse in the conventional position, with the *male on top of the female.* There is, I think, some kind of mystery surrounding this theme of *heterosexual cunnilingus.* Men are usually quite surprised to find that women prefer this above all other sexual activities, and women are surprised that men don't find it almost as stimulating as they do. It is also possible that women think that men enjoy performing *cunnilingus* because men tell women this in order to please them. I am not suggesting that men actually *lie* about their enjoyment of this activity, but they may, after viewing how enjoyable it is to a woman, express a greater appreciation of it than they actually feel, just as women do when performing *fellatio.*

Heterosexual Intercourse, Male on Top of Female

Men ranked *heterosexual intercourse, male on top of female,* as number 9 in their sexual preferences. Women estimated it for men at a close number 10. Females were only one point away in estimating where men would rank it. In contrast, men were nowhere near as accurate in predicting how women would respond to this theme, predicting it as woman's number one preference. Somehow women know that men do not find this sexual activity as stimulating as their practice of it would indicate. I think this stems from some adolescent associations with intercourse that carry over into adult life. For the adolescent male, intercourse means "doing it"—getting on top of a girl and "sticking it in." This becomes almost the primary obsession of the majority of young, inexperienced males. Their female partners begin to understand and accept this as a natural male drive. Most first sexual experiences take the form of intercourse with the male on top of the female. These early associations often interfere with more mature sexual needs and drives and affect both sexes. Women, however, on some level are more aware of these dynamics. As this data reveals, they do not make the assumption that what a man performs sexually is necessarily what he prefers sexually. We know that women do not find intercourse in the conventional position as stimulating as other activities, yet men make the assumption that this is what women prefer. By remaining silent women have insured that the cycle of noncommunication will continue.

Heterosexual Petting, Partially Clad

Men ranked this activity as number 10. Women estimated it for men at a somewhat higher number 7. The fact that women were close in predicting the accurate male ranking of this theme, but erred in predicting that men would rank it higher than they actually did, may indicate that women are working from experiences they had in adolescence. When petting with clothes on is all that is available to a young man, he obviously responds to it with enthusiasm and fervor. A woman who predicts that males would rank this as a high priority may be recalling the extreme degree of excitement that a male showed when he first saw an exposed breast or was permitted to explore a partially clothed female body with his hands or mouth.

Sadomasochism, Male on Female

Men ranked *sadomasochism, male on female,* as number 11 in their sexual preferences. Women estimated it for men at number 16. What is surprising about this data is the extremely low estimated rank that women, who are taught to assume and accept male aggression, projected for men. Women actually felt that men would rank this theme lower than *anal intercourse between two males.* In actuality, men find it somewhat, if not highly, stimulating, having ranked it just one point below the top ten preferred sexual activities. I think this rather dramatic discrepancy stems from a woman's incomprehension of why a male would find the rape fantasy appealing. She knows it is appealing for her because she can then feel totally possessed, totally overwhelmed, totally without responsibility. Women apparently cannot see that a man can be turned on by putting himself in the position of a rapist. From a woman's point of view, there would be no real need for a male rape fantasy; a man can have any woman he wants. I think, however, that when a healthy male identifies with the rape situation, he thinks primarily of acting upon natural aggressive impulses, of being totally in control. We have talked about how women have historically had the role of "gatekeeper," of directing and controlling potential sexual situations by saying no. As Nancy Friday's study of male sexual fantasies confirms,[4] men have developed some anger, even rage, over the fact that women through their learned roles reject male sexual interest. Consequently, men feel a loss of power over women and their own sexual urges. In showing a preference for *sadomasochism, male on female,* males are expressing their need for a channel of release for the disappointment and anger that female rejection creates. What the results of the study have shown is that, in the range of human sexual needs, there exists a wider diversity of attitudes, behaviors, and responses than might ever have been supposed.

Female Masturbation

Men ranked *female masturbation* as number 13. Women estimated it for men at a rather high number 5. Here is another large discrepancy between what men actually ranked and what women predicted they would. Obviously, women feel that men find *female masturbation* much more highly stimulating than they actually do. It is possible that women may have heard of pornographic films that portray a masturbating woman, and assume that men like this because it is part of pornography. The assumption is usually that the woman is sexually stimulating herself in preparation for intercourse with a man. The pictures that were used in the study depict this theme as women using their fingers or dildos to bring themselves to orgasm, and not really requiring any additional assistance. This may be the reason why men tended to rank this theme as low as they did. There is a very moving scene in the film *Last Tango in Paris,* where a woman masturbates in the presence of her lover. Far from being excited, the male is sitting in the corner weeping. The implication is that there is an absence, a loss of contact and intimacy in the relationship, for which he is feeling some grief. Also, and this recalls the male response to Shere Hite's suggestion to women that, in order to receive optimum sexual satisfaction, they "do it themselves,"[5] men simply do not like the idea that women can be sexually fulfilled without them. It is important to recognize that women can tolerate and be stimulated by a man satisfying himself; they ranked *male masturbation* tenth. Men, however, seemingly have much more trouble conceiving of the idea that women can attain pleasure on their own.

Homosexual Anal Intercourse

Men ranked this activity as their least preferred, number 19. Women estimated it for men at a somewhat higher number 15. Although women know that male homosexuality is not stimulating to men, they were apparently unaware of just how low on the scale of alternatives men rank this theme. Society has said to heterosexual man that homosexual intercourse is one of the worst sins he can commit. It violates the social and natural order, according to the rules of convention and propriety. Women, unaware of the intense power of this message to males since they do not experience a similar message about their relations with other females, ranked this theme as the least stimulating to themselves. They felt, however, that males would find something in it to allow them to rank it higher than the least stimulating theme.

We can see from the data presented in this chapter that there is a range of accuracies and inaccuracies in the participants' attempts to predict the sexual preferences of the opposite sex. While there were a number of accurate predictions, such as females' ability to predict males' preference for *fellatio* and males' ability to predict the excitatory value of the *nude male* for females, there were also some inaccuracies.

Men, for example, predicted that females would prefer missionary sex as their number one choice, and they had no idea of how stimulating the *triad* was to women. Females, on the other hand, were way off base in estimating how exciting the *female superior position of intercourse* and *sadomasochism, female on male,* were to men.

What is fortunate about the results of this data is that there are some activities that each sex prefers and that the opposite sex shows considerable interest in these. This information should be shared between the sexes so that we can begin to work toward a more genuine, natural model of sexuality and rid ourselves of the impositions and frustrations of conventional, authoritarian forms of training. Obviously, whatever forms of sex education our society has developed have not been effective in preparing adults to completely understand the opposite sex.

Males need to be encouraged to learn and understand more about females. Females need to be encouraged to learn and understand more about males. And both men and women, as the results presented in the next chapter will show, need to begin to feel comfortable in identifying with the specific dynamics of their own sex.

6 Sexual Speculations: How Men and Women Perceive Same-Sex Preferences

TABLE 5 (*continued*)

Theme	*True Female Rank*	*Female Estimated Rank for Females*
Heterosexual intercourse, male on top of female	6	1
Sadomasochism, male on female	7	12
Nude male	8	8
Heterosexual fellatio: oral sex, female on male	9	5
Male masturbation	10	10
Homosexual fellatio	11	18
Sadomasochism, female on male	12	13
Partially clad male	13	9
Homosexual cunnilingus	14	15
Nude female	15	14
Female masturbation	16	11
Homosexual petting, female	17	17
Partially clad female	18	16
Homosexual anal intercourse	19	19

WHAT THE RESULTS MEAN

Heterosexual Cunnilingus: Oral Sex, Male on Female and Heterosexual Intercourse, Male on Top of Female

Women ranked *heterosexual cunnilingus* as number 1 and *heterosexual intercourse, male on top of female,* as number 6 in their sexual preferences. They estimated these for other women at numbers 2 and 1 respectively. I have chosen to discuss these two themes together because they are obviously related in the female mind. While women knew that they themselves preferred *cunnilingus* above all the other activities presented as sexual alternatives, and while they guessed that other women would rank it a high second, women still assumed that other women would prefer the most conventional form of sexual activity, intercourse with the man on top of the woman. It is interesting to observe that women often proved much less conventional in their thinking when they were asked to predict what men would prefer sexually. They did not fall into the traditional assumption that men would naturally choose intercourse in the "missionary" position over all other activities—as the men did in predicting female preference. Challenging this assumption with their experience, intuition, and knowledge, women predicted that men would opt for *fellatio.* Given their own sex, however, women seem to be reluctant to state that other women would choose a sexual activity as their number one choice that is still often regarded as deviant. Again, women remain extremely sensitive to the social desirability of sexual behavior and appear to make their predictions of what other females prefer on this basis rather than on what they know to be their own preferences. Women are so conditioned *not* to trust their own feelings and instincts about sex that even when they know for themselves that a particular sexual activity is exciting, they have no confidence in their ability to predict that the activity would be stimulating to other women as well. Women rely more on the voice of authority and convention than on their own feelings and flesh in predicting other women's responses to unconventional sexual activities. This principle also applies in female estimates of the next theme, the *triad.*

Triad: Two Males and One Female Joined Together and Engaged in Coitus and/or Oral-Genital Activity

Women ranked this activity as number 2 in their sexual preferences. They estimated that other women would rank it at number 7. By admitting that their own individual choice would be to rank the *triad* much higher than they would expect other women to, women are revealing to us that they have some trouble trusting the validity of their own fantasy worlds and, when asked, opt for the intervention of what they consider the "real" world of conventionality and recognized medical authority. Even though an individual woman may fantasize making love with two men, who can take care of a number of physical needs that one can't, she obviously fails to realize that this would be as appealing and attractive to other women. She apparently feels that she is alone in wishing for this type of situation, and makes the assumption that other "normal" women would demurely choose a much more restricted and conventional situation as sexually stimulating. Women can't believe that this is a shared fantasy among women, although the results of this study indicate that it most definitely is.

The Foreplay Themes: Heterosexual Petting, Both Nude, and Heterosexual Petting, Both Partially Clad

Women ranked *heterosexual petting, both nude,* as number 3 and *heterosexual petting, both partially clad,* as number 5 in their own sexual preferences. They estimated that other women would put these at numbers 4 and 6 respectively. Women have no difficulty in accurately predicting the stimulating value of foreplay, for themselves and for other women. This theme may be one of the rare ones actually discussed among adolescent females. It is accepted as a healthy interaction between males and females, and women obviously do not feel that there is anything wrong with them or with other women in acknowledging it as one of their most preferred sexual activities. The enormous popularity of romance novels where invariably sex begins and ends with a kiss seems to verify this finding.

Heterosexual Intercourse, Female on Top of Male

Women ranked this activity as number 4. They estimated that other women would rank it number 3. In closely predicting the high erotic value of intercourse with the female in the superior position, women are, I think, making judgments that are actually based on their own physiological responses, not on what they think is culturally acceptable. The woman who takes the aggressive role in having intercourse with a man, who straddles his penis while on top of him, knows that this is more physically stimulating than the conventional form of intercourse because there is more direct contact with the clitoris and vagina. Also, when a woman is in control of the sexual act, she directs her movements so that her own bodily pleasure can be significantly increased. She is also in a better physical position to request fondling and sucking of her breasts, which heightens the sexual stimulation of intercourse.

Sadomasochism, Male on Female

Women ranked *sadomasochism, male on female,* as number 7 in their own sexual preferences. They assigned it a lower number 12 for other women. This was a significant discrepancy between actual and predicted female rankings. Women felt that other women would find this activity much less stimulating than they found it themselves. Just as one woman would be hesitant to reveal to another woman that she had rape fantasies, so here a woman finds it difficult to believe that other women would find highly stimulating an activity that could be regarded as demeaning and diminishing. The important point is that women feel alone in these desires. They feel that wanting to be totally possessed by a male who puts them in a position of utter vulnerability and passivity is somehow unnatural. Women do not assume that other women have these same needs, yet, as the study indicates, other women obviously do.

Nude Male

Women ranked the *nude male* as number 8 for themselves, and estimated that other women would also rank it a number 8. Women, just like the men, were exactly accurate in predicting how sexually stimulating a *nude male* is to a female. This is a much more likely topic of conversation among women today, especially now that the media appears to support the idea that women can enjoy looking at men's bodies just as men can enjoy women's. It would be much more comfortable for women to discuss with one another their aesthetic responses to a picture of a *nude male* than to reveal intimacies regarding their paticipation in specific sexual activities, and, therefore, women are able to predict with much more accuracy the appeal of this particular theme.

Heterosexual Fellatio: Oral Sex, Female on Male

Women ranked this activity as number 9 in their sexual preferences. They estimated that other women would rank it at a higher number 5. We know that females are aware that *fellatio* is the number one sexually preferred activity for men, because they so accurately predicted it. It is probably for this reason that women guess that other women would prefer to engage in this activity—more than they actually do. It is difficult for a woman who is operating from the premise that other women want to please men to believe that they would rank *fellatio* lower than, for example, *heterosexual petting, partially clad.* Women share an unspoken assumption that they are aware of how stimulating *fellatio* is to a man and that they will, in order to please him, engage in this activity. A woman who ranks this activity ninth, as most women did, would then feel that she was unusual in not complying with her role of pleasing men and predict that other women would rank it much higher. In this case, women probably know what other women prefer only indirectly, on the basis of what men communicate to them. A man may express to a woman that she should try *fellatio* because another woman, or a threatened other woman, has tried it and loved it. Having no real frame of reference that would allow her to confirm or dispute this claim, a woman supposes that other women are very different from herself. In the novel, *A Chance to Sit Down*, one of the characters expresses this confusion:

> "The trouble is that sexually one is so isolated, not from the opposite sex, but from one's own. It isn't the jealousy, it's the terrible insecurity of it, the fear of what she does with him that I don't."[1]

Male Masturbation

Women ranked *male masturbation* as number 10 for themselves, and estimated that other women would also rank it at number 10. They were exactly accurate in predicting the erotic value of this activity for other women. Like the nude male, this is a more objective point of reference for female communication. A masturbating male is erect and in some way preparing himself for orgasm, whether with or without a partner. In acknowledging this theme as one of their top ten preferences, women apparently find no threat here to their own self-image.

In the remaining themes, there were dramatic discrepancies between actual and estimated rankings in *homosexual fellatio* and *female masturbation.* As we have seen women actually found *homosexual fellatio* fairly stimulating, ranking it only one point below the top ten. Other females, however, thought that women would rank this theme second to last. It is possible that when women were ranking their own individual preferences, they responded specifically to the nude male body and the erect penis with heterosexual interest. When estimating what other women would rank this theme, they may have focused more on the general negative associations that surround male homosexuality.

On the other male and female homosexual themes, women were fairly accurate in predicting the degree of stimulation each theme would hold for other women. They were also within one point of accuracy on the themes of *sadomasochism, female on male,* and *nude female.* They were far less accurate in predicting the excitatory value of the *partially clad male* and *female masturbation.* It is surprising that women thought that other women would rank *female masturbation* much higher than they actually did, given women's negative cultural conditioning concerning the exploration of the female genitals.

THE MALE VIEW OF MALE SEXUALITY

In general, males were better able to predict the sexual preferences of other males more accurately than females were able to predict the sexual preferences of other females. We generally think of men exchanging sexual attitudes and opinions in locker room conversations and through such media as the *Playboy Advisor*. While this may be true, apparently men are not communicating about the themes that are most often thought of as "abnormal" or "deviant." Men were also way off in predicting the excitatory value of some conventional themes such as *heterosexual intercourse, male on top of female*, the *nude female* and the *partially clad female*. Men were, however, quite accurate in predicting how low other males would rank homosexual themes.

TABLE 6
Male Estimates of Male Preferences for Sexual Activity

Theme	*True Male Rank*	*Male Estimated Rank for Males*
Heterosexual fellatio, oral sex, female on male	1	2
Nude female	2	7
Heterosexual intercourse, female on top of male	3	3
Heterosexual petting, both nude	4	5
Partially clad female	5	10

TABLE 6 (*continued*)

Theme	*True Male Rank*	*Male Estimated Rank for Males*
Triad: Two males and one female joined together and engaged in coitus and/or oral-genital activity	6	8
Sadomasochism, female on male	7	14
Heterosexual cunnilingus, oral sex, male on female	8	4
Heterosexual intercourse, male on top of female	9	1
Heterosexual petting, both partially clad	10	6
Sadomasochism, male on female	11	12
Homosexual cunnilingus	12	11
Female masturbation	13	9
Homosexual petting, female	14	13
Homosexual fellatio	15	16
Partially clad male	16	18
Male masturbation	17	15
Nude male	18	17
Homosexual anal intercourse	19	19

WHAT THE RESULTS MEAN

Heterosexual Fellatio: Oral Sex, Female on Male, and Heterosexual Intercourse, Male on Top of Female

Men ranked *heterosexual fellatio* as number 1 and *heterosexual intercourse, male on top of female,* as number 9 in their own sexual preferences. They estimated these for other men at number 2 and a surprising number 1 respectively. It is very interesting that males followed the exact same process as did women in estimating their own sex's ranking of oral-genital contact as opposed to heterosexual intercourse in the conventional position. Although individually men ranked *fellatio* as the most stimulating sexual activity (as women individually ranked *cunnilingus* as the most stimulating sexual activity), and individually ranked heterosexual intercourse in the conventional position as relatively low (as did individual women), men believed that other men would prefer the most commonly practiced form of sexual activity —*male on top of female*—more than any of the other alternative sexual activities, and then would choose *fellatio* second. Women followed exactly the same pattern with their predictions of how other women would rank heterosexual intercourse in the conventional position and *cunnilingus.* Somewhere in our heads, and this includes both sexes, we are convinced that intercourse in the missionary position is the world-favored activity and that we, ourselves, must be completely alone in preferring oral-genital sex or any other activity.

Nude Female

Men rated this as number 2. They estimated it for other men at a lower number 7. It seems difficult for males to accept the fact that other males have been as preconditioned as themselves in responding to photographs of nude women. Given the variety of sexual activities that the men were asked to rank and predict, men apparently believed that other men would naturally prefer an activity where two people are sexually involved as more stimulating than the *nude female*—even though individually they ranked the *nude female* as more stimulating than any other sexual activity except *heterosexual fellatio*. In this society, pictures of nude women have come to represent SEX, and men respond to this association. They experience an extremely high erotic stimulus from viewing pictures of (or viewing real) nude women. They do not appear to be aware, however, that this is a general response of men who are raised in this culture. In addition, arousal at the sight of a nude body is an admission of the kind of undifferentiated lust that we discussed in Chapter 2. Males are much more likely to separate a sexual stimulus from an emotional relationship than are females. The fact that men were hesitant to think that other males would find this appealing may indicate that some individual males feel that they are alone in their experiences of undifferentiated sexual impulses.

Heterosexual Intercourse, Female on Top of Male

Men ranked *heterosexual intercourse, female on top of male,* as number 3 for themselves. They estimated for other men also at number 3. Men were exactly on target in predicting how sexually stimulating other men would find intercourse in the female superior position. This is no doubt a theme that is available for communication among males, and they are in agreement about its excitatory value. It is also probably not a topic of discussion between men and women, as women were unable to predict that men would be highly excited by intercourse in this position. Women thought that men would rank it ninth.

Heterosexual Petting, Both Nude

Men ranked this activity as number 4 for themselves. They estimated it at number 5 for other men. Of all the themes, the foreplay themes seem to be the ones that both men and women agree are important to themselves and to the opposite sex. In contrast to Shere Hite's claim that men care only about their own orgasms, the male ranking of this theme, as well as the male prediction of how other males would rank it, indicates that men put a high premium on *petting* and find it is a stimulating activity.

Partially Clad Female

Men ranked the *partially clad female* as number 5 in their own preferences. They estimated it for other men at a significantly lower number 10. Males were unable to predict exactly how exciting a *partially clad female* is to other men, and the reasons seem to be similar to those behind their inability to make accurate predictions about the excitatory value of the *nude female* theme for other men. Men merely assume that other men prefer sexual activities that involve a partner to the experience of looking at a *nude* or *partially clad* woman. Even though the individual man finds himself becoming very excited by this theme, he may feel that other men would feel that he was not fulfilling the *macho* role that society has imposed upon him.

Triad: Two Males and One Female Joined Together and Engaged in Coitus and/or Oral-Genital Activity

Men ranked the *triad* as number 6 in their own sexual preferences. They estimated for other men at number 8. Men came fairly close to an accurate prediction on this theme. They did, however, slightly underestimate the excitatory value that two men and one woman can hold for males. We have previously discussed the reasons why this might be. I do believe that if the photographs on this theme had depicted two women and one man, both the male ranking and the male predictions of male ranking would have been considerably higher.

Sadomasochism, Female on Male

Men ranked this activity as number 7 for themselves. They estimated it at a much lower number 14 for other men. Here again, we have a dramatic example of how the process of acculturation can limit the perspective of individuals who are being asked to evaluate their own and others' sexual preferences. Individually, men find this theme quite exciting and erotic. It is seemingly very appealing for a man to be allowed to take the passive role, to give up expectations of aggression and power in the sexual situation. In our culture, however, men are taught that to do this is to be a "sissy" or "mama's boy" or a "queer." They are taught to think that they must be in control of all situations at all times. This is a very heavy burden, and may be why individual men find the idea of being sexually passive so sexually exciting. For once, they can permit someone else to take over. Men cannot, however, feel that other men would permit and allow themselves this kind of freedom from responsibility. The discrepancy between how males actually ranked *sadomasochism, female on male,* and what they predicted other men would rank it is a significant statement of how an individual can, due to external demands, reduce and deny his own sexual needs, desires, and freedom.

Heterosexual Cunnilingus: Oral Sex, Male on Female

Men ranked *heterosexual cunnilingus* as number 8. They estimated that other men would put it at a higher number 4. Men predicted accurately that women would rank this activity second and perhaps they felt that there should be enjoyment among men of an activity so clearly favored by women. One of the shockers of the entire study is this discrepancy of rankings and predictions on the themes of oral-genital sex. Men may not have felt comfortable predicting that other men would rank a theme that women found stimulating so low, but, as we have previously discussed, this topic of *heterosexual cunnilingus* appears to be somewhat mysterious for both sexes. The following chart demonstrates the wide variations between actual rankings and estimations for both sexes.

Heterosexual Cunnilingus

	Male	*Female*
Male estimate of preference	4	3
Actual	8	1
Female estimate of preference	2	2
Actual	8	1

It is important to recognize that the male ranking for *heterosexual cunnilingus* as eighth and the female ranking as first does not mean that women are either doomed to frustration about this activity or doomed to begging their male partners to perform it. While a ranking of eighth is not the highest, it does reflect that males find *cunnilingus* highly sexually stimulating. It is in the top ten of their sexual preferences. Men do prefer some other activities, for example, *fellatio* and the *nude female*, but they still find *cunnilingus* an exciting and satisfying activity.

In the remaining themes, men were fairly accurate in predicting the excitatory value of male and female homosexual themes for other males. They were, for example, only one point away in predicting the value of *homosexual cunnilingus* and *homosexual fellatio.*

Men overestimated the sexually stimulating value of *heterosexual petting, both partially clad.* This is probably because males tend to associate this theme with adolescent fantasies, as it represents the most commonly practiced activity in adolescence. Men may have believed that other men would still find this theme highly stimulating.

Men also overestimated the value of *female masturbation* for other males. This is most likely due to the fact that a popular theme in "girlie" magazines is an enticing female who is looking down at and getting ready to fondle her genitals. Men have frequent exposure to this particular theme and probably assume that other men would find it exciting.

The results of the data on same-sex predictions validate what I have said earlier in the book—that conventional training and attitudes generate a great deal of confusion in the area of communication between and within the sexes. One of the most illuminating discoveries of the study is the unfortunate failure of individuals to accurately predict the preferences of their own sex. The implication is that people have not been taught or encouraged to trust their own feelings and instincts.

Had men been able to say, for example, "I would like to be tied down and acted upon by a woman, so probably other men would too," the discrepancy between the actual and the estimated ranking of *sadomasochism, female on male,* would not have been so wide for males. Similarly, had women felt comfortable with being excited by the *triad,* there would have been a much higher percentage of correct guesses on predicting the very significant preference for that theme.

I think that one of the ways individuals who participated in the study were able to transcend some of the limitations of their own sex training and sexual experience was to employ the technique of fantasy. By looking at the pornographic pictures of other adults engaged in activities that the individuals themselves may never have practiced or performed, both men and women were able to identify with what that experience might be like without actually taking the risk of engaging in the activity.

It is quite probable that women who chose the *triad* as their second most preferred activity had never experienced a sexual situation involving two men. It is also quite probable that men who revealed a preference for *sadomasochism, female on male,* had never been tied down by a woman. Yet they were able to fantasize what such an experience would be like and, through the process of fantasy, make some important discoveries about their own sexual preferences.

We definitely need to get more in touch with our real sexual feelings. Men need to know that what the culture has taught them is mandatory sexually is not necessarily what is most pleasurable sexually. Women need to free themselves from the severe restrictions that their early training imposes upon them and discover what is most naturally sexually fulfilling. Once we understand our own sex, we can make some advances in understanding the opposite sex.

I am reminded of a recent experience with a patient of mine who reported to me that she was also seeing a marital counselor. Both she and her husband were going to this counselor because of some rather severe marital difficulties, including sexual ones.

My patient, whom I will call Anita, had been brought up in a very strict, conservative home where the topic of sex was never raised. She had had sex only twice before she married, and she found real difficulty in feeling free and sexually expressive in the marital relationship.

Her husband had complained that she was "frigid," even though she had had orgasms on several occasions. His definition of frigidity was that she was unwilling to try any new forms of sexual activity, especially oral sex. Anita's position was that while she had often yearned to experiment with more stimulating and less conventional sex with her husband, she had great difficulty in admitting these desires to him as they embarrassed and humiliated her.

During a session with the male marital counselor, Anita admitted these feelings of reticence and guilt. His response was this: "Anita, haven't you ever let the little whore in you come out? Every woman has a little whore in her that wants to come out."

Anita was so upset by this remark that she ran out of the counseling room and, when she next saw me, spent an entire session talking about it. For her, the counselor's use of the word "whore" confirmed her own feelings that she must be "bad" or "naughty" to have sexual impulses. While he was trying to let her know that her feelings were natural and that most women had them, his choice of terms had merely added to her sense of guilt and shame.

Had Anita had some frame of reference that would educate her in the sexual feelings, desires, and behaviors of other women, she would not have felt so completely isolated in the process of realizing her own. She would have been able to acknowledge her feelings as part of her female sexuality rather than "whorish."

Anita's story is an unfortunate illustration of the rather dismal state of affairs in the communication of the sexes. Not only do we have trouble comprehending the nature and needs of the opposite sex, but we are quite frequently left with no relevant context or standard within which to place our own. Anita had no appropriate feminine standard by which to judge her sexual desires and curiosities. At a time when she needed to express them in a supportive and accepting climate, she found herself thrown back on early training experience that judged these feelings as negative and degrading.

What Anita and, perhaps, all of us need is an opportunity to relearn some of these feelings and to place them in a positive and growth-producing atmosphere. In the following chapters, I will present some ideas on how we can "relearn" our own sexuality, how we can discover new alternatives, new options for sexual attitudes and behaviors. I hope this material will provide readers with the same opportunity that is available to individuals who enter into psychotherapy—that necessary and revitalizing "second chance."

Individuals in therapy are given a second chance to work through those areas of their lives that they have developmentally missed or distorted. In the next chapter, we can learn to rework and alter those areas of our sexual lives that we have missed or distorted. We can try to change the old and discover the new, to develop ways that allow us to embrace our sexuality free from guilt, self-consciousness, and cultural expectations that thwart our human needs and responses. Now that you have read about and experimented with discovering your own and other's sexual preferences, it will seem more comfortable to begin to look at these new ways to express, define and create your own patterns of sexual communication and behavior.

7 Where Do We Go From Here?

THERE is no question that sexually we are a society in limbo. Until the last two decades of this century, children and adults had everything fairly well defined. They knew what was considered to be right, what was viewed as wrong, and what lay between. Now it seems as if everything lies in between. Without clear boundaries or defined guidelines for behavior, we are sexually where Matthew Arnold once placed the nineteenth-century world religiously: "Struggling between two worlds, one dead, the other waiting to be born."

This is not an easy task. We have been given lifelong training in accepting the restraints of social convention, and it is difficult to find ways to transcend what we have unquestioningly accepted in search of something new. Probably the most significant obstacle to forging new conventions is the wide variety of alternatives that the sexual revolution has generated. What bothers most of the people with whom I talk is the overwhelming number of options they perceive as available to them. Apparently people fear that if they were to exercise these options, the result would be utter chaos.

Somehow many people equate the necessity of sexual restrictions with that of legal restrictions. Changing sexual conventions seems, in their minds, equivalent to allowing motorists to choose which way to pass ongoing traffic on the basis of individual whim rather than according to law.

I am reminded of a patient of mine who was terrified to be left alone for any extended period of time. Her fears were grounded in the belief that, with no one around to supervise and control her, she would overindulge herself by eating as much candy as she wanted. She felt the need to have specific limits set upon her, obviously feeling incapable of setting limits for herself.

That is what most people I talk with today express about sexuality. They are afraid of their own freedom. They don't know where the limits are and they are desperately seeking some set of rules to provide them with reasonable boundaries for behavior. Unlike the analogy of the driver who chooses willy-nilly whether to pass on the right or the left, responsible individuals can make choices about their sexual attitudes and behavior that will not result in social chaos.

Men and women can develop for themselves a comfortable moral code that is not based simply upon what their parents taught them, nor on civil or biblical law. We do not need to escape from our own freedom in fear of chaos or candy. We can put ourselves in the driver's seat and determine which roads we want to travel and how we can avoid colliding with others who choose to travel different ways.

In this chapter, I would like to present some specific examples of how couples using the knowledge they've gained by learning about sexual preferences in this book can begin to look at ways to relearn attitudes and behavior and develop a sexuality based on a structure of real needs rather than on a structure of societal demand and expectation.

I know a number of couples who are "stuck" with the old sexual messages that they heard throughout their childhood and adolescence. Let me use the example of Judy and Allen, a couple who came to me for therapy. This couple demonstrates the radical differences in the way boys and girls are taught to view themselves and the unfortunate legacy this can leave in adulthood.

Allen was twenty-five, a rising engineer in a large corporation, and had been married to Judy for three years. Judy was twenty-four and had been working for an advertising firm for five years. She first came to see me because of a negative body image that was affecting her marriage. She said that she had never felt comfortable with her body and that she had trouble allowing Allen to look at it, let alone explore it.

Even though Judy was talking to a female therapist about this problem, she had difficulty in maintaining eye contact with me when she mentioned anything connected with her own body or with sex. She reported similar difficulty with Allen, and complained of their mutual inability to discuss sex or any issue of physical intimacy. Judy admitted that she had never experienced an orgasm, and it was clear, given her difficulties in sexual communication, that Allen was unaware of this problem.

After seeing Judy for five sessions, I suggested that Allen be included in the next one. When Allen began to talk about his background, Judy felt more comfortable in discussing hers, and some of the important issues that were obviously separating them began to surface.

First, it became apparent that Judy and Allen had been taught to cope with their physical and sexual growth in adolescence in radically different ways. Allen expressed very positive feelings about the appearance of pubic hair in his genital area and on the chest. He commented that he felt lucky to have developed pubic hair early, as some of the other boys that he knew felt great embarrassment over not being so fortunate.

Allen also remarked on being able to take some pleasure in the marked physical changes of adolescence—the broadening of the shoulders, the growth of hair on his face, chest, and genitals, and the deepening of his voice. He said that he began to feel that he was changing from a boy into a man, and that when he was thirteen, the gifts and acclaim that accompanied his Bar Mitzvah seemed actual confirmation of his physical entry into manhood.

Judy sat and listened to Allen in stunned silence. When I asked her how she felt about what he was saying, she replied with one word: "Envy." When encouraged to talk, Judy explained that all she could remember about her own physical development was shame and guilt. She recalled feeling very uncomfortable when her mother with some embarrassment suggested that they go out and shop for bras. She also said that she felt "fat and ugly" (if I had a dollar for every time I heard a female use this phrase in describing her feelings about herself, I would be a rich woman) when she realized that her breasts and hips were developing.

When I asked Judy if she were able to talk with anyone, her mother or a friend, about these feelings, she replied that she would have been much too embarrassed. "My mother made me feel that my body was a source of embarrassment to her, to me, and to everyone else, even though she never actually *said* that." About talking to friends, Judy said, "I just assumed I was the only one who was feeling like this; all my girl friends seemed so much more attractive than I."

Judy was an unfortunate victim of what might be called an "ancestral curse." That is, her mother, along with thousands of other mothers, obviously felt some discomfort about her own physical development and processes and, in some way, communicated this embarrassment to her daughter. It is no secret that mothers historically have had trouble in talking to their daughters about sexuality, as Nancy Friday's very popular *My Mother/My Self* so dramatically confirms.[1]

Judy also suffered from feelings of isolation and loneliness because she felt that no one else felt the same way she did. When she expressed this point, Allen volunteered some very interesting information about how males cope with sexual feelings. He said that when he first began to feel sexual urges, he, too, felt alone. Then he began to talk to some of his friends, who reassured him that his feelings were normal.

He also told us that a very important aid in sharing information and feelings with his friends was the "eight-page bible." Most women, Judy and myself included, would probably tell you that they had never heard of an eight-page bible. Certainly no comparable item has been available for females. The "bible" is a small comic-book publication covertly put out in high school print shops. Typically, the pages of a bible will present cartoon drawings of nationally known male figures like movie stars, comic strip characters, or politicians, engaging in various sex acts.

Allen reported that these little publications serve as convenient tools of communication for young men by relieving some of the anxiety and fears that adolescent males experience about their developing sexuality. They are able to laugh over the artist's depiction of Dick Tracy inserting a ridiculously large penis into an eager and passionate female partner who has an absurdly enormous bust. This kind of humor and distortion of sexuality makes males much more able to cope with the nervous energy that surrounds their sexual feelings. They can share it with members of their own sex in an atmosphere of fun and laughter.

This is in dramatic opposition to the somber silence that women share over issues of developing sexuality. While males are sharing information about their sexual feelings and telling each other dirty jokes to relieve some of their nervousness about sex, females sit in stony isolation, developing feelings of guilt and shame about the fact that they are becoming sexual and, therefore, "bad."

Judy reported that sex was never discussed in her middle-class home, but that she picked up very clear messages during her adolescence that made it plain to her that only "bad" girls had sexual feelings and indulged in heavy petting and intercourse. Before meeting Allen, Judy had had no sexual experience except masturbation, which, as she later expressed, carried severe associations of guilt and shame.

Judy's lack of premarital sexual experience brought up yet another significant difference with Allen, and one that had a direct affect on their marital sexual relations. Allen came from a family that was predominantly paternalistic. He was taught to value "being a man" and to respect women, especially his mother and four sisters. Allen learned that he had some social permission to explore his sexuality; in fact, he commented, "I think my father expected it of me."

Allen's first sexual experience occurred in his junior year of high school with a girl whom he slept with only twice. His subsequent sex education was obtained from prostitutes and a few high school girls who were notoriously "loose." When Allen met Judy, he responded immediately to what he called her "innocence," and he made no sexual demands on her during their premarital relationship.

This situation created a conflict in Allen that is shared by many men. We have previously discussed the issue of sons learning quite early to put their mothers on pedestals of purity that deny them any real and valid access to the dynamics of female sexuality. Allen learned that his mother and his sisters were to be put into one group of females and that the women he slept with were to be put into another.

Obviously problems arise when a man tries to connect the females of one group with the females of the other. If mother is "nice" and "innocent" of the realm of sexuality, then any female involved with sex must be "not nice." You can imagine Allen's dilemma when he fell in love with and married Judy, whom he perceived as "innocent" and also took to bed.

As Judy and Allen discussed their backgrounds and attitudes, it became increasingly apparent that some sex difficulties between them were inevitable. They were both, in many ways, victims of their upbringing. They were brought up in a world where sexual values were not individualized and communicated but rigid and suppressed. Allen was given a male prerogative for sexual exploration but no opportunity to learn about female sexuality. He knew about women only from what he heard other males report and from what he experienced sexually with women who were promiscuous or prostitutes. He was learning to devalue women who expressed their sexuality.

Judy was given no support for her developing femininity and this caused her to suspect and deny her own sexuality. She was never taught to appreciate her developing body as a source of sexual stimulation, nor was she given any opportunity to ask questions, the answers to which might have provided some comfort and relief from her increasing anxieties and fears.

The result of these contradictory learning experiences was, for both Judy and Allen, a set of marital and sexual problems that could be resolved only through therapeutic help. Their therapy required that they work through some of the issues that they had previously taken for granted. Judy had to acknowledge the negative attitudes she had about her body and her sexuality and begin to appreciate them as positive assets. Allen had to realize the conflict he had over "good" and "bad" women and begin to accept Judy's new interest in and enthusiasm for sex as a tribute to their relationship.

Both began to understand the importance of time and learning together. Judy had been asked to remain indifferent to sex until she married, at which time she found that she had developed so many "blocks" that she was unable to enjoy sexual expression. Allen had been taught that men knew everything about how to make a female sexually happy, but found that he succeeded only in making Judy feel guilty and frustrated. They learned that these feelings and attitudes do not change overnight, and that they had to make a commitment to helping each other change by shared communication. With a deeper understanding of themselves and each other, Judy and Allen were able to develop a very successful sexual relationship. This intimacy transferred over into a number of areas in their personal lives, and they found themselves communicating on new levels.

Judy and Allen's problems of sexual inhibition and frustration stemmed from early social and cultural conditioning experiences. Sometimes individuals suffer from being exposed to sexual events or situations for which they are not yet prepared. This premature exposure may cause sexual inhibitions that are just as firmly ingrained as those experienced by Judy and Allen, and may severely limit the range of one's sexual exploration.

When one of my patients was eleven years old, she came across a series of pornographic pictures portraying oral sex between men and women. Even though her mother had prepared her for a general and vague recognition of sex through a brief and stilted discussion of the "facts of life," this eleven-year-old child was hardly ready for the onslaught of information she received while looking at these particular pictures.

As an adult, this patient completely withdrew from any activity involving oral-genital sex. The first time her partner approached her with the suggestion, she was horrified and experienced physical manifestations of shaking and severe stomach pain. With the help of therapy and an extremely understanding and communicative sex partner, she was able to work through these fears and false projections, understand their cause, and, ultimately, be able to enjoy both cunnilingus and fellatio.

This same process of negative conditioning by premature exposure to a sexual event was an inhibiting factor for another couple, Kim and Carl, who came to me in therapy. When I first saw Kim in therapy, she complained of physical pain in her stomach. She reported that this pain usually started when she saw her husband nude or with his genitals partially or fully exposed. Her discomfort did not prohibit her having intercourse, but it did have a rather dramatic effect on the limits she would impose on lovemaking.

Kim would not, for example, allow Carl to make love to her in the daytime, and she stipulated that no lights be on at night if they were going to have sex. Kim also intimated to Carl that he should never walk around nude and should always be clothed in at least a robe.

At first, Carl assumed that these "rules" related to Kim's desire for decorum, and so he went along with her wishes. As time passed, however, Carl began to observe that, whenever by chance Kim did see him in the nude, she would register a look of disgust. He began to see that the situation was severe enough to require help, and so he suggested that Kim enter therapy.

Through the course of my work with Kim, we discovered that as a child she had frequently been exposed to her alcoholic father's semi-nude body, particularly his hairy chest and genitals. When Kim's father was drinking, he often walked around the house in his undershorts and revealed, intentionally or not, his genitals. This was a source of extreme upset and humiliation to Kim, especially during adolescence when she would have friends or dates over and would never know just when her father might appear in this unseemly attire.

Kim had begun to view the male body as disgusting because her first experiences of it occurred at a time when she was completely unable to absorb it in any positive context and under conditions with many negative associations. She also developed guilt based on the feeling that she should not have looked at her father when he was in this state.

During the course of her therapy, Kim began to realize that the physical feelings she experienced with Carl were the same feelings that she had experienced over her father's slovenly and seductive exposure. I felt it would be helpful for Carl to join in on some of the therapy sessions, and, eventually, Kim became comfortable with sharing this information about her past and how it was directly affecting their personal life in the present.

Carl was understanding and supportive and, through the combination of his help and therapy, Kim began a process that allowed her to become more responsive to and accepting of her husband's body. Gradually she started to explore and look at parts of Carl's body, beginning with his arms. From Kim's perspective, these were safe, and quite muscular and angular. In time she began to experience Carl's arms as sexually appealing and exciting.

Eventually they moved on to other parts of Carl's body, his legs, chest, even his genitals, until Kim was able to appreciate Carl's entire nude body as stimulating and sexually attractive. They began to make love in the daytime, which increased Carl's satisfaction, as he was especially stimulated by viewing the nude female body.

In Kim and Carl's case, therapy was necessary to eliminate a fundamental block to a couple's sexual freedom and fulfillment. Kim's exposure to her father's nude body had severely limited her capacity to respond as a sexual adult female. Once she began to understand the source of her negative feelings, she could begin to develop new, positive associations and then she was able to accept and appreciate her husband's body and to respond to it.

Therapy is not always necessary in allowing a couple to overcome some of their limitations in sexual exploration and satisfaction. A couple can find their own methods and means of liberation without any direct therapeutic support. A good example of this comes from Doug and Susan, a couple both of whom had participated in the study on sexual preference.

I had occasion to meet Doug and Susan socially a few months after they participated in the study. Doug approached me, reminded me that he had taken the test, and said: "I want to thank you for what you did for us." I was somewhat surprised, as it was my perception that my participants had actually done a great deal for me.

He commented that both he and Susan had enjoyed taking the test and that afterward they had compared and discussed their responses. They found themselves questioning each other on what were the most sexually stimulating themes for them individually. Doug implied that these discussions radically transformed their sex lives.

As I never enter into professional discussions on an individual's or a couple's sexual experience while socializing, I asked them if they would mind making an appointment to see me at my office so that I could get from them some much-needed feedback on how the study had actually affected their personal sexual relationship.

During two meetings with them, I gathered some very interesting information. This couple found that, after participating in the study, they were able for the first time to have discussions about sex outside the confines of the bedroom. They were able to sit comfortably in their living room or kitchen and communicate to each other some of their own feelings about the sexual themes involved in the study. This new freedom was delightful to them, and they found themselves joking and laughing together and able to remove sex from a context that established it as "serious."

Both of them loosened up considerably during these discussions and found that there was a new element of play in their communication. Doug would coax and cajole Susan into expressing what it was that really turned her on, and Susan would pretend coyness and shyness. Doug would respond with statements like "Take a chance, love, what have you got to lose?" and Susan would come back with "My husband! He may think I'm perverted!" They both admitted to me that through this playing they were able to persuade and "court" each other into revealing their most intimate sexual preferences.

One of the most stimulating themes for them was the *triad*. When they finally got around to admitting this to each other they were both delightfully surprised, even slightly shocked. Susan confessed to having fantasies about another man being in the room with them while they were having sex. It is important to recognize that Susan insisted that she would never actually allow this to happen, and that she definitely wanted to remain monogamous. The fantasy, however, of having another male observe her activities with Doug was extremely exciting to her, and these feelings were aroused when she had looked at photographs representing the *triad* during her participation in the study.

After Susan's expression of the preference, Doug confessed that he had often experienced fantasies of another man making love to Susan while he himself looked on. He had felt somewhat guilty and embarrassed about these feelings, but they had most definitely been aroused when he viewed photographs of two men and one woman in the study. Doug realized that what really excited him was fantasizing that Susan would make love with another man for a brief period of time and then Doug would join them, at first engaging in oral sex and eventually in intercourse.

You can imagine how revealing and important this shared information was. They began to envision that they could incorporate their individual fantasies into their lovemaking with no threat of outside competition. Doug did not view Susan as promiscuous because she had these fantasies, and Susan did not see Doug as perverted or any less sexually interested in her. They saw these fantasies as material they could use to enrich their sex life, and they decided to utilize them.

It is important at this point to underscore the very significant line that exists between fantasy and reality. Fantasy serves as a way to engage the power of the mind and imagination to get in touch with responses that can then increase and deepen the actual experience and communication. It is a technique that can work as well for a couple as for an individual.

Susan and Doug both reported to me that their conversations about their own fantasies were highly stimulating to them, particularly because they took place when they were not actually making love. There was an element of anticipation and excitement that pleased them both. The first time they made love after sharing these feelings was, in Susan's word, "fantastic" and in Doug's "incredible." I very much appreciated their willingness to share this experience with me, and I will try to describe it as accurately as they did.

Doug initiated the lovemaking by taking Susan into the bedroom and saying, "Let's pretend there is another man in here." He then moved her toward the bed, very slowly undressing her, and describing aloud a situation he was making up in his head. He began by telling Susan that they were in a hotel and had previously met a man at the bar who had seemed very attracted to Susan. Susan responded immediately by describing the man to Doug, emphasizing those characteristics about him that were sexually appealing to her. Doug then told Susan that he had invited the man up to their room for a drink, and that he would be arriving shortly.

Then together they began to fantasize what would happen. Susan suggested that they would all have a drink together. Doug, who was still in the process of very slowly undressing Susan, decided what they would talk about (obviously, sex) and how soon after the discussion the other man would join them in sex, at first merely observing and then eventually participating.

By this time Doug and Susan were on the bed, Susan was undoing Doug's belt, and both of them were actively engaged in the fantasy. Doug began to make love to Susan by asking her what she would like the man to do. Susan expressed that she wanted the man to stroke and suck her breasts, which Doug then did. They continued to fantasize in this way, all the while incorporating the fantasy into their actual lovemaking by Susan's requests of the imaginary man and Doug's willing compliance. Doug also at times took the initiative by whispering to Susan what he thought the man would do next: "and then he'll stroke your leg, put his finger in your vagina, put his penis inside you, etc." Susan got increasingly excited and involved by asking, "And what will he do then, and then?"

Both partners expressed the feeling that they considered this process highly erotic and, in fact, utterly engaging and believable. Doug felt that he was both an observer and a participant and Susan felt that she was being made love to both by another man while her husband observed and by her husband while another man observed.

They also admitted that this form of sex play did not become their only method of sexual communication. It existed to them as an option that they could use whenever either or both of them were in the mood. Their way of expressing to each other that they were ready for the *triad* fantasy was for Susan to say to Doug, "Tell me a bedtime story" or for Doug to ask Susan, "Do you want to hear a bedtime story?" They both told me that this fantasized experience added a wonderfully enriching dimension to their marital sex life, which remained monogamous.

The important first step for Doug and Susan was to admit and express to each other their own sexual fantasies, to accept them without threat or guilt, and then to begin creatively and imaginatively to utilize their mutually shared preferences to increase their sexual communications and enjoyment together.

Another couple, Tom and Marlene, neither of whom participated in the study, benefited greatly from familiarizing themselves with the study's results. At a speaking engagement where I discussed each of the sexual themes presented in the study, a woman approached me, and, like Doug, thanked me for opening up new sexual awareness and activity for her.

Marlene told me that she was an avid reader of Rosemary Rogers, whose novels are often referred to as "soft porn." This author frequently uses erotic restraint, or, as it was termed in the study, *sadomasochism, male on female.* Marlene was highly excited by these passages. Her husband, Tom, often questioned her about why she purchased so many of Rogers's books, but Marlene was extremely shy about revealing to him that they provided her with a sexual turn-on. After hearing me speak and learning that many females found this theme to be sexually stimulating, Marlene gained courage and decided to approach Tom with this information about her own sexual preference.

Fortunately, the experience of new-found courage occurred during a summer vacation when Marlene and Tom's two children were away at camp, and Marlene felt even freer to, as she put it, "spice up the routine" than she would under more ordinary circumstance.

One evening after dinner, Marlene started to tell Tom the results of my study. Again, as with Doug and Susan, this was a "first" in that they had never shared a lengthy discussion of sex outside of the bedroom. Marlene said that while she and Tom were able to express interest in having sex to each other while, for example, watching television, they never actually discussed their individual feelings or preferences for sexual activities.

Tom expressed more interest in this particular discussion than Marlene had anticipated. He began to ask her directly what she found to be most sexually stimulating. Marlene, somewhat taken aback, and for a moment feeling less courageous than at first, replied, "That's a very personal question."

Marlene's response is an example of a phenomenon that I have observed in many women: they will find themselves aroused by a book, an event, an experience, and will fantasize acting out this sexual feeling with a man, and yet will avoid and, at times, deny any expression of this sexual feeling to the partner involved.

What occurs in these incidents is the unfortunate replay of childhood and adolescent learning that tells a female that any direct expression of interest in sexual exploration and experimentation, especially if it is in areas that are not conventional or socially acceptable, is akin to, in the words of our recently quoted marriage counselor, "letting the little whore out."

Tom, fortunately, was not about to let this matter drop, and he began to pursue the issue by asking numerous questions such as, "Which one is it? Will you tell me if I guess? Have we ever done it?" Making very little headway with this line of inquiry, Tom finally said, "All right. I'll tell you which theme *I* like most." He then admitted that one of the themes that really turned him on was *female masturbation.*

Marlene was completely surprised, and began to ask Tom to tell her why this was so and asked if he would enjoy watching her masturbate. This discussion stimulated both of them and succeeded in allowing Marlene to reveal to Tom that what most stimulated her was what the study termed *sadomasochism, male on female.* Tom looked at her with shock and curiosity and said, "You mean beating, with chains?" Marlene assured him that her fantasy did not stretch to painful coercion, but only to the desire to be restrained and in bondage while being made love to.

This was a totally new form of communication for Marlene and Tom. They had never before discussed such topics. All conversation about sex had previously been limited to the subject of how much foreplay should occur before intercourse. They were seeing each other in a new light and finding that they totally enjoyed this new and surprising dimension of their relationship.

One of the most liberating results of their discussion was that they both admitted to practicing and enjoying masturbation. Marlene confessed that she would occasionally masturbate when excited by reading a novel and had been reluctant to tell Tom this because she felt that he might feel undermined in his sense of manhood if he knew that, at times, she could please herself.

Tom reassured her that this was not the case and encouraged her to talk about her feelings. He, in turn, admitted that he engaged in masturbation during those times when Marlene was unavailable to him, particularly just before and after childbirth.

Marlene later expressed to me that there had been a great deal of laughter between them in this discussion because they had both been convinced that the other would regard masturbation as perverted or disgusting when, in fact, their mutual admission of practice and enjoyment of this activity brought them very close together.

The next opportunity that Tom and Marlene had to make love, Tom asked Marlene if she would really like to be tied down. She admitted that she would love it but was afraid that she would constantly be thinking about a fire breaking out and would be anxious about her safety. Tom's solution, like Doug's, was to use fantasy in satisfying his partner's sexual preference. He asked her to pretend that every place he touched her was "tied" or "bound," and he began by squeezing her wrist, putting it above her head, and saying, "There, I just tied your arm down. You can't move it." He then grabbed her other wrist, squeezed it, and confirmed that her other arm was now tied. He proceeded to do the same with each ankle, making sure, in the process, to remove Marlene's panties.

Marlene was extremely excited by this, and began to move those parts of her body which were not "tied down." Tom then began to make slow and passionate love to her, and, each time Marlene would move an arm or a leg that had been mutually considered "bound," Tom would squeeze it tightly so that she would be reminded of her "restriction."

Marlene was able to completely accept this imaginative bondage as believable, and to gain from it an extraordinary amount of pleasure and sexual gratification. As with Doug and Susan, Tom and Marlene did not perform this as their single subsequent sex activity, but it became one of an increasing number of sexual options.

Judy and Allen, Kim and Carl, Susan and Doug, Marlene and Tom all had problems, whether individually or as a couple, with inhibitions that developed as learned responses. For Judy and Allen, inhibitions arose from the ways that they had been taught to view their own and the opposite sex and from a rigid and restrictive sexual upbringing. Kim had developed a negative association with the male body because of premature exposure to her father's body. Susan and Doug and Marlene and Tom had made some rather inhibiting assumptions about what they should or should not prefer sexually. Each of them had to relearn and rework their sexual attitudes and behavior.

By exposing themselves to the unfamiliar, the new, the unknown, these couples were able to become comfortable with sexual attitudes and behaviors that were ultimately very satisfying. They did not have to remain restricted and limited by their past learning and conditioning on sexuality. Through the power of imagination and mental energy, they were able to free themselves and, through dialogue and communication with their partners, reawaken their natural instincts and desires.

I once heard a psychiatrist comment that the most important sexual organ was the brain. This observation is extremely relevant here, as it confirms the power of intelligence, imagination, and fantasy in bringing about a change in the way an individual can learn to relate and respond to sexual experiences and events that he or she has previously considered bad or forbidden.

I suggest that you now return to the results of the test that you took on your own sexual preferences. Review the themes you found to be most stimulating, even if, as is quite probable, you have never engaged in them. Attempt to put yourself and your partner into this activity, either in fantasy, in reality or both. Feel and think how it would be to perform this activity. Try to discover ways you would feel most comfortable in engaging in the activity. In familiarizing yourself with those themes that you found most stimulating through fantasy, you can become more ready both to discuss and to practice them with your partner. You can begin to free yourself of any prejudgmental approach that has in the past limited or inhibited your natural responsiveness.

In my speaking engagements, I often refer to the song that was popularized by Charlie Rich, "Behind Closed Doors." The song reinforces the idea that, within the four walls of the bedroom, or whatever private sanctuary you and your partner may choose, you have the right to experiment with and perform any activity you both feel comfortable with. Nobody except those directly involved in the activity knows what you and your partner choose to do or not to do.

Couples who take responsibility for their own sexual preferences will attempt to incorporate them into their sex lives through the use of communication, fantasy, and imagination. This liberating process will leave people more trusting of their ability to establish personally gratifying sexual boundaries and more tolerant of other's sexual behavior and less uptight about options.

Such a process, of course, is fine for the generation of adults. In order to really change society, however, human beings will need to discover how to begin the process of learning about sex in a positive and constructive climate. To really free ourselves from this sexual limbo, adults must begin to rethink methods of teaching children about sexuality and to develop new models of learning that will eliminate the problems and hang-ups they themselves experienced.

8 New Options

THE sexual limbo discussed in the last chapter has brought with it a new, if sometimes confused, sexual emancipation for adults. We cannot, unfortunately, assume that this emancipation in adult sexuality necessarily brings with it instant and responsible sex education to prepare children for the new freedom that they will discover.

In fact, many recent studies have shown that parents are extremely uneasy about the new sexual environment. They know that they cannot rely on the old rules, but they have not adopted any new ones. What usually happens is that the confused parents remain silent about sex, and refrain from dealing with their children's curiosity about sexual matters.

In 1978 the Harvard-based Project on Human Sexual Development published a "Kinsey-type study" on parental guidelines for children's sex education.[1] Out of a sampling of 1,400 parents, researchers found that between 85 and 95 percent stated that they never discussed intercourse, masturbation, or contraception with their children. Less than 50 percent had discussed menstruation, even with older daughters. The survey also revealed that more parents tacitly approved of premarital sex for sons than for daughters. And those parents who did claim to explain issues of sexuality with their children considered one conversation to be sufficient.

Another survey, conducted at Johns Hopkins University by Laurie Schwab Zabin, John F. Kanter, and Melvin Zelnik, confirmed that sex-education programs are offered too late to help adolescent females.[2] The researchers interviewed 526 women who were eighteen to nineteen years old at the time, and who had become pregnant at least once before marriage. The results revealed that the majority of females wait at least one year or more after beginning sexual activity to seek information on birth control. It also suggested that public opposition to sex education was largely responsible for the one million annual teenage pregnancies in the countries.

As a society we are in the position of wanting to prevent teenage pregnancies and abortions but finding ourselves apparently unwilling to teach children how to avoid them. In our silence about sex we are expressing deep fears about the effects of early reproductive education, that is, of giving children information about sexuality before they become sexually active. The thinking seems to be, "If a kid knows about it, then he/she is going to do it."

In a study conducted by the Merrill-Palmer Institute of Detroit, Dr. Greer Litton Fox explored the relationship of 449 fourteen- and fifteen-year-old girls with their mothers.[3] Dr. Fox discovered that mothers are the most critical influence on their daughters' sexual behavior. She added: "Our data suggest that a mother can do no harm by talking to her daughter at a young age, at ten or eleven, about the mechanics of sexual intercourse and birth control."

It is apparent that we must begin to think in new ways about educating our children in sexuality. The freedom that the sexual revolution has brought to us should be accompanied by increased parental responsibility in teaching our children how to handle it. The more parents begin to openly discuss sexuality with their children as a fact of life, the better the chances of raising healthy, well-adjusted adolescents and adults.

Many parents are reluctant to embark on sex education with their children in part because of the difficulties and ambivalences that occurred in their own. A good example of this comes from an incident in my own personal life. When my daughter was about six years old, she and I were in the bathroom while I was putting on makeup and she was taking a bath. She reached down to her genital area and found her clitoris. She asked, "Mommy, what is this part of me called?"

My first reaction to her question was a tightening of my body and an impulse, fortunately not acted upon, to yank her hand away. My reaction was not based on maternal instinct; it was based on learned behavior. I was responding purely from an attitude that had been internalized by old messages that I had received during my own childhood. Running somewhere through my head were phrases like "Naughty, naughty, don't touch" and "nice girls don't do that."

Since we had already discussed the term *vagina,* I could have opted for an easy out by saying, "That's your vagina, remember?" This would have allowed her to remain ignorant of the distinction between the vulva, labia, vagina and the clitoris and, thereby, join the ranks composed of vast numbers of American women.[4]

Something, however, nudged me to explain more fully. In a relatively calm voice I said, "That's your clitoris, which is nearby but different from your vagina. It feels good when you touch it." Part of the old messages stayed with me, however, because I added: "We don't touch that part of ourselves when we are in public."

To begin properly, parents must develop an attitude of approval and acceptance in all areas of a child's developing sexuality. This does not mean that parents need to condone whatever the child chooses to do sexually. It does mean that the emotional and physical implications of sex should be seen as positive and valid parts of the total sexual self. These must be acknowledged and accepted by the parent as he or she simultaneously attempts to provide the child with information that is necessary for the development of a healthy and positive perspective on his or her sexuality.

I do not mean to suggest that this is going to be easy. Given parental background and experience, it will mean that an entirely new set of sexual options and behaviors and opinions must be formed. As the poet Rilke says: "Sex is difficult; yes. But they are difficult things with which we have been charged."

As a starting place, we might attempt to discuss our sexual attitudes with the parent or partner who is sharing responsibility for the sex education of our children. Everyone is capable of creating for him- or herself and for the family a series of options and alternatives to traditional methods of sex education, most of which are presently nonexistent. One of the ways to start is to employ, as did the couples we discussed in the last chapter, imagination and fantasy to determine what the best words and explanations would be in your own individual situation.

In the following pages I will attempt to provide a framework of ideas on some sex-education issues that may come up in the family setting. I cannot give you an exact script that will work beautifully for every parent-child situation. I can give you a general structure to use to begin to make your own discoveries and to determine what course you choose to take.

I urge you to note this important consideration: Never do anything you feel uncomfortable with. Advice on sexuality is hitting us from all quarters, and some is better suited to some people than to others. I happen to believe that the advice I am offering is reasonable and sensible. If, however, it is not right for you, then discard it for something that works better.

Since we are trying to establish new and different norms of acceptability in sexual matters, I think it is very important to begin talking to children about them as soon as the children are ready. I have observed children as young as three or four to be concerned about their body and their physical development. At this age, they are fairly comfortable with asking a variety of questions about many areas of life. If you are satisfying their curiosity in other areas, it is relatively easy to begin talking with the child about what is happening to his or her body and how this will affect future development.

Parents who are sensitive to the continuing questions and concerns expressed by children between the ages three and eight have a very good foundation for a healthy communication with the child during the difficult prepuberty and adolescent years. Once the early communication is established, it is far simpler to continue comfortable and honest conversations into the later years. It is essential that parents realize that one conversation is *never* enough. It has to be a continuing dialogue that grows and changes with the cognitive, emotional, and physical development of the child.

A very good opening ploy is for the parent to offer positive feedback on the present state of physical development the child has achieved. All children like to be told that they are progressing normally, that they are, in comparison with their peers, "all right." The old-fashioned yardstick markings on the kitchen wall are good indicators to a child that he or she is growing at a good and normal rate. If this measurement is begun early, when the child can understand the concept of growth, and when it is accompanied with positive parental comments, then both parent and child have established a sound basis for communication on body development and physical growth and change.

It is important that parents respond to sexuality not only on a physiological level by explaining anatomy and reproduction, but also on a personal level that acknowledges that sexuality is pleasurable and physically satisfying.

I think it is unfortunate that traditional forms of sex education have focused on the differences between male and female anatomy, described as if solely for purposes of reproduction. This type of training is valid and important, but it is not enough. It is only one half of the picture.

Each reproductive part of the body has a dual function: physiological and pleasurable. What I am calling for is the acknowledgment of this very important second function so that children can begin to be comfortable associating their developing sexual body with their increasing sexual desires and needs. By providing specific recognition and approval of the pleasurable dimension of sexuality, the parent can help the child to develop a sense of achievement and growth that is directly related to the enhancement of the sexual self. I will stress the importance of this concept throughout the discussion to follow.

One very important way that parents can help their children to understand and appreciate their sexuality is to make a special point of responding to a child's sexually developing body. When, for example, a girl of eleven is found exploring her breasts in a mirror, she is giving her parent an excellent opportunity to provide her with information as well as share feelings about her body in terms of how it will relate to her future womanhood.

A parent's first response may be, "I see your breasts are developing nicely and you will soon be ready for a bra." This may encourage the child to ask questions like "Why do I have breasts?" "Why don't boys have breasts?" or "What are breasts for?"

The parent can then develop a dialogue with the child by saying something even as simple as: "The development of your breasts is part of what happens to you as you become a woman. Breasts are a very beautiful part of a woman's body. They are soft and round and lovely to look at." The mother then may take the opportunity to express some of the positive feelings she has about her own breasts. It is important to communicate a sense of pride and appreciation for this totally physical and pleasurable dimension of female sexuality.

It is also good to encourage the child to express her own feelings about her bodily growth. Asking questions such as, "How do you feel about your breasts?" may give the parent a very good idea about the child's self-image. If, for example, the girl responds by saying "I'm embarrassed because I'm the only girl in my class who has them," the parent can relieve some of the anxiety behind the statement by explaining that the child is simply maturing more rapidly than others in her age group and that it is only a matter of time before other girls catch up. The parent can also comment on how physically attractive the child's breasts have become and emphasize that she should feel pride and accomplishment rather than embarrassment and humiliation.

When a parent is able to open up discussions and dialogue in this way, it becomes relatively simple to answer questions related to physiological growth and physiological function. In explaining how breasts relate to future womanhood, a parent can respond to a girl child who is wondering why she has breasts that she will be able to use them to feed babies. The same principle applies to any discussion the parent and child will have about menstruation: the process of shedding blood is directly related to the female's ability to conceive a child.

Similar types of discussions can occur with a male child. For example, when a boy shows interest and concern about pubic hair or penis size, the parent can help out by encouraging him to ask questions. "Why do I have so much hair all of a sudden?" and "My penis gets hard sometimes" are issues that every developing male experiences, whether he verbalizes them or not. The parent can give the child positive reassurance about the progress of the child's development by saying, "You are becoming more of a man, and your body is developing very well. You are handsome and attractive, and someday you will be able to pleasurably use your penis to help make babies with your wife."

These types of parent-child conversations, if handled properly in an atmosphere of open acceptance, can literally transform what might be an adolescent's nightmare into a very positive learning experience that fosters growth, change, and understanding. All too often adolescents associate their developing bodies with feelings of fear, shame, and embarrassment.

We are considering how the physical manifestations of sexual development can be transformed from objects of shame and begin to be appreciated as necessary realizations for healthy and normal adult sexuality. Some of the specific issues that I am asked about most often in discussions of adolescent growth are masturbation, menstruation, premarital sex, and opposite sex and single sex parenting.

A frequent concern of both parents and children is masturbation. Masturbation is a topic that can potentially bind parents and children together in their attempt to communicate about sexuality. And, of course, it is an activity that almost every child experiments with at one time or another. If a child is found "playing with" his or her genitals, a parent can look upon this as an opportunity to acknowledge the physical need and explain to the child that this kind of self-exploration and experimentation is normal, natural, and acceptable.

If the child begins to feel that the parent is accepting of his or her natural urges and impulses, the child is much more likely to feel free to express sexual feelings and concerns. When the eight- or ten-year-old has discussed masturbation in a climate of comfortable acceptance with the parent, he or she will most likely continue to refer to it when it arises in discussions during the teenage years. I have often suggested to parents that they openly converse with their children about viewing masturbation as an alternative to sexual intercourse during the years thirteen to seventeen, when the desire for sexual activity is quite intense.

The adolescent is generally caught between the intensity of physical desire and the negative social sanctions against masturbation. This is a problem that can be solved by enlightened parental attitude and approach. Parents should openly discuss the positive effects of masturbation with adolescents: it provides a healthy physical release of sexual tension with none of the harmful and negative by-products of sexual intercourse; it can allow the individual to indulge in what might be "unacceptable" fantasies with no harm to anyone else; it can provide a "practice" or "rehearsal" function so that later sexual activity can be more comfortable and enjoyable.

What we are striving to accomplish is to break the silence and negative associations that surround sexuality in the parent-child encounter. In doing this, parents should always try to present sex as an integral part of life rather than a mysterious and/or forbidden intrigue. Adolescents need a lot of help with their developing sexuality and they need this help even before their sexuality begins to surface. If children are prepared in prepuberty for some of the feelings and experiences they will undergo as adolescents, they will be better able to incorporate these into their lives and to view them free of feelings of guilt, embarrassment, or abnormality.

Menstruation remains perhaps the most taboo subject in this difficult dialogue that we are trying to establish between parents and children. Both sexes suffer from the myths and ignorance that surround the topic. It was hardly encouraging when I spoke recently to a man of forty-five who told me that when he was sixteen and learned that his sister had begun to menstruate, his vision of the process was that "her bleeding was like peeing" or, in other words, something like a faucet.

Many men retain an attitude of fearful ignorance about menstruation. Perhaps this willful ignorance is why most fathers greet their own daughters' menstruation with such remoteness. Over and over again in my therapeutic and personal conversations with women, I hear about their perception of their fathers and the other male figures intimately connected with their lives as being completely distant from anything relating to menstruation. Menstruation is a female experience that most women have been taught to hide from men.

Only when menstruation is treated by the whole family as the beginning of womanhood will the onset of a female's period be viewed as cause for family approval and support. In order to hasten this day, I suggest to parents that they begin discussing menstruation with both boys and girls very early, around nine or ten years old. I urge that the father be included in any discussion of female menstruation and the mother in father-son explanations. I also urge that both parents make a specific point of explaining the function of menstruation so that boys and girls can begin to understand that menstruation is a normal physical function directly related to conception and birth.

We should also begin to ritualize and celebrate the onset of menstruation in much the same way that a male's entry into puberty is celebrated as, for example, in the Jewish tradition of the bar mitzvah. We need to imagine ways in which a child's entry into womanhood can be heralded and celebrated rather than hushed and pitied.

In many of my speaking engagements, I have suggested that a father who has been in open and comfortable discussions with his daughter about menstruation and other topics of sexuality send his daughter a bouquet of flowers on the day of her first period. As a rule this suggestion is greeted with surprised delight from both male and female members of the audience. This gesture would provide the father with a means to express his male acknowledgment and approval of his daughter as a woman, as well as a vehicle of recognition that menstruation is a positive process in female sexuality.[5]

The bouquet of flowers and perhaps a special family dinner could represent respect, support, and appreciation that could make a world of difference for the female adolescent. Instead of feeling that she has now joined the ranks of cursed womanhood (many women still use the term "the curse" in explaining menstruation to their daughters), this fortunate female could enjoy feelings of pride, accomplishment, and anticipation.

If the girl has brothers, it would certainly be meaningful for them to be included in this occasion of family celebration, not only to reward their sister, but also to begin to develop and understand positive associations with menstruation. The entire experience should be one of family sharing, a sense of communal exchange between parents and siblings that reinforces the positive feelings that should surround this significant event in a female's life.

A recent study has shown that women who in later life suffer from severe menstrual discomfort report that very negative feelings surrounded their first experience of menstruation.[6] If this negative learning can have such a powerful effect on a woman's future physical and emotional life, then we can hope that replacing the negative learning with some positive affirmation might have long-lasting consequences in transforming a female's attitude about herself and her womanhood.

Another explosive topic that should specifically be addressed in parent-child conversations on sex is premarital sex. I know that many parents fear talking about premarital sex with their children because they "don't want to give them any ideas." We have to face the fact that teenagers already have plenty of ideas and that most of them are acting them out.

The statistics of teenage pregnancies are staggering. Studies show that one in ten unmarried teenage girls become pregnant each year. This means that there are more than one million pregnancies, 600,000 births, and more than 300,000 induced and 150,000 spontaneous abortions *each year.*[7]

There has been a historical decline in the age at which teenagers lose their virginity. In the 1950s Kinsey reported that 3 percent of females and 40 percent of males lose their virginity by age sixteen. At the age of nineteen, 20 percent of the females and 72 percent of the males had experienced sexual intercourse. In 1973 a report showed that 30 percent of the females and 44 percent of the males in a representative sample had lost their virginity before the age of sixteen.[8] I think we can assume that this age decline is still continuing.

There is no question that we must find ways to bring responsible education to teenagers on the topic of premarital sex. We have already learned from a previous study that sexually active girls usually wait to seek out information on birth control until they have been having intercourse for a year or more. This means that a large number of girls are vulnerable to pregnancies while in their early and middle teens. Parents must learn to confront that fact and to try to take steps to control it.

When mothers ask me if I condone premarital sex, I usually ask them what age they are talking about. Premarital sex between mature young adults is one thing; premarital sex between immature teenagers is another. In my speaking engagements I often make a statement that shocks many women. It is this: "A mother of today who raises her daughter to feel good about herself, good about her body, and good about sex cannot expect her to remain a virgin until marriage."

This statement, so surprising to many mothers, is not an advocation of promiscuity nor an advertisement for premarital sex. It is a statement of fact that calls for a distinction between responsible and irresponsible sexual activity before marriage.

Parents too often neglect to teach their children this important distinction or wait until it is far too late. It is particularly those parents who are concerned about their child's sexual activity during adolescence who should have begun preparing the child with information on intercourse and birth control before the child starts to experiment with sex. More importantly, these parents should be prepared to place sexual activity in an emotional context. They should discuss with their child such subjects as the meaning of love, the connection between intimacy and love, and the question of responsibility, commitment, and ethics in love.

This provides the parent with a means to acknowledge the emergence of a child's sexuality, along with a way to stress the necessity for waiting for emotional maturity. Parents can provide supportive guidance in helping a teenager cope with the temptations of premarital sex by carefully explaining to their children that because they are not yet emotionally prepared for sex, they are vulnerable to being deeply hurt. They do not yet understand what it means to love, nor the caring and commitment that responsible loving demands. They are not, then, prepared for sexual intercourse, which accompanies that kind of loving.

I cannot stress strongly enough the importance of the parent's establishing an early open dialogue about sex in order to provide this kind of guidance for the adolescent heading toward the emotional liabilities of sexual activity. If a parent can begin explanations early, before the child hears the distortions that come from conversations with other children or from interpretations of silence, he or she is much more likely to get signals that a teenager is contemplating entering a sexual relationship.

In households where parents have treated sex as a secret, so will their offspring. Then the parent will learn about a child's sexual activity only when trouble arises. Unfortunately, this is too often the case. From my experience with parents of teenagers, very few of them are willing to discuss emotional issues with their children. They fear that the child may interpret this kind of conversation about the emotional side of sexuality as the parent's resigned acceptance of teenage sexual activity. This need not be the case if the discussion is handled properly.

It is, as I have said, very important to communicate to children your understanding that they too have sexual impulses and needs. The parent can make it clear that to understand is not, however, to condone. Parents of those adolescents who express, either covertly or overtly, interest in beginning a sexual relationship should make it clear that, at the ages of fourteen, fifteen, and sixteen, teenagers are not emotionally prepared for sexual involvement.

There is a vast difference between the adolescent, especially the female adolescent, who engages in sexual activity at fifteen and the young woman who does not remain a virgin until marriage. I think that many parents could possibly accept the fact that their daughters may choose to have sexual relations with a partner when they are eighteen or nineteen and involved in a serious relationship. They would probably have a great deal of difficulty, however, accepting this behavior in a daughter of fourteen or fifteen.

This was confirmed by the results of a study that

I mentioned earlier in this chapter which found that mothers who had daughters of fourteen and fifteen years of age tended to disapprove of any sexual activity for their daughters.[9] Only 10 percent of the mothers said that sexual intercourse was acceptable for their daughter of this age, and these made the stipulation that their daughter be "in love." The *Redbook Report* revealed that girls who begin sexual activity at fifteen are more likely "to have many sexual partners before marriage, to have extramarital sex after marriage . . . and to be less happy in general and in their marriages."[10]

There are valid reasons why adolescents of fourteen and fifteen should not enter into sexual relationships. There is no question that early teenage relationships are much less painful to sever when no sexual involvement has occurred. Once sex comes into the picture in a teenage relationship, words like "love," "commitment," and "future" tend to be misused and abused. Younger teenagers are not ready to attach proper and relevant meanings to these terms. They find themselves in the position of having the experience and missing the meaning. This makes the loss of the relationship, which at age fourteen to sixteen is almost inevitable, confusing and difficult to bear.

There is often a sense of guilt in a young adolescent female when a relationship that has included sexual intercourse dissolves. She may feel that she was being used or manipulated. For the young adolescent male, there is always the problem of the bruised and battered ego. The breakup of a premature sexual relationship may suggest to him that he lacks the virility and potency the girl desires. Since the young teenager has not yet established a strong enough identity to suffer sexual rejection, he or she will almost certainly feel some sense of violation of self.

Parents who understand this will do their children a great service by explaining the emotional issues of sexuality and the reasons why a young teenager should not engage in sexual activity. This does not, however, mean that, because the parent has discouraged sexual relationships, there is no need to give the child information about birth control.

As I have said from the start of this discussion, I think it is extremely important for parents to give children birth control information, not only before they begin sexual activity, but *before they are able to reproduce.* A child's understanding of intercourse, reproduction, and birth control needs to develop. He or she will not immediately and accurately understand the entire process the first time it is presented. Children will process information that is given them according to their mental and emotional abilities.

This means that parents need to introduce information at an early age, repeat it during developmental stages of the child's growth, and ask questions to make sure that the child has actually heard the material and taken it in. Parents who wait to give their children any information about the reproductive process and birth control until their children reach puberty are in danger of expressing an easily misinterpreted two-sided message.

On the one hand, they are saying, "Now that you are capable of fathering or conceiving a child, I don't trust you." On the other hand, they are implying by belatedly sharing what has previously been privileged information that now they are giving their sanction for sexual activity. Neither of these statements is consistent with the parents' best interest or with the message they want to convey.

A good example of how parents can express contradictory values and attitudes about birth control is cited in Aaron Hass's *Teenage Sexuality.* A sixteen-year-old girl reported this incident in her own experience of parental guidance:

> My mother first told me that if I ever needed any form of contraception to go and talk to her about it. The next day, straight out of the blue, she said if she ever found out that I was pregnant or having sex that I shouldn't step foot in the house again.[11]

Another young teenager, a fifteen-year-old girl, expressed considerable emotional turmoil over an attempt to discuss contraception with a parent:

> Once I asked my mom that maybe it would be a good idea if I took the pill in case I am in a situation and I can't get out of intercourse. My mom thought I was giving her a bull story and I was already having sex. That surprised me because I was telling the truth, and I cried.[12]

The way to avoid the risk of these contradictions and misinterpretations is to bring up the topic of birth control as early as you bring up the topic of sexual intercourse and human reproduction. This should occur before the child is struggling with intense sexual impulses. Teenagers deserve to be made aware of possible consequences and precautions long before sexual performance is an option.

As must be abundantly clear by now, I feel strongly that an ongoing and continuing dialogue concerning the topics of sexual development, masturbation, menstruation, premarital sex, emotional intimacy, and commitment, accompanied by information about birth control, is the best preparation for sexual maturity that a parent can give a child. But this flow of communication becomes increasingly effective when both mothers and fathers adopt responsibility for the sex education of both daughters and sons. When we consider that for the vast majority of people sexual experience takes place with members of the opposite sex, it becomes apparent that the opposite-sex parent would have a very strong advantage in helping his or her child to understand his or her own sex.

One of the purposes of this book is to increase the communication between the sexes. Therefore, it seems quite relevant to ask: "How can we expect men and women to feel comfortable talking to each other about their sexual needs and desires when, as a child and an adolescent, they have discussed sex with only their own sex? And, because there is no discussion of sex with a member of the opposite sex, how can we expect men and women to regard each other as anything but mysterious and unavailable for sexual communication?"

From the data obtained by the *Family Life and Sexual Learning* study conducted in 1978, it appears that few parents do any kind of sex training at all. Aaron Hass reports that out of a sampling of 625 teenagers between the ages of fifteen and eighteen, 66 percent of the boys and 65 percent of the girls claimed that they could not be open with their parents about sex.[13]

When sex education does occur it is usually accompanied by feelings of awkwardness and embarrassment. Typically the father takes the son off to talk about the "facts of life," while mother takes the daughter into a room to discuss what it is to "be a woman." This split between the sexes, occurring as it does at an age conducive for learning, does more to alienate females and males than to help them understand each other.

We have previously discussed the ways in which children are taught to view the parent of the opposite sex. Little girls learn that their fathers are usually remote and unavailable. They assume that sex is a topic that is not to be discussed with father, even though they may sense that he would be critical and punitive if he were to learn that his daughter was sexually active.

Young males are taught that their mothers are to be protected and removed from the reality of sex, that they are pure and innocent creatures whose asexuality saves the world from the predominance of male lust. Adult males often encourage their sons to withhold information about their physical developmental needs from their mothers, justifying this concealment by the fact that "Mother is above all that."

How often have we, as adolescents and even adults, expressed to someone the dismay we felt when we learned that in order to have children our parents must have "done it"? If, as in the natural process of child development, we have made an identification with the parent of the same sex, then we can also imagine that they have sexual needs similar to our own. An adolescent female can project her own sexual desires and fantasies onto her mother, as an adolescent male can imagine that his father has sexual impulses and needs. The reason that most of us find it so difficult to believe that our parents would actually engage in intercourse together is that we have never been taught to perceive the opposite-sex parent as a sexual being.

This means that most of us grow up thinking that the opposite sex is unavailable for sexual information, communication, and expression. One of the major reasons for this is that the first male that girls have as a sexual model, the father, is often remote and uncommunicative about sex, and the first female that boys have as a sexual model is a mother whom he is taught to put on a pedestal and separate from any of the realities of sex.

Another major reason is the fear of incestuous feelings between opposite-sex parent and child. The classical psychoanalytic view is that the onset of puberty renews the childhood feelings about one's parents.

Incestuous fantasies of an adolescent are more troubling than those of a young child because in adolescence incest would be physically possible.

Some theorists suggest that incestuous fantasies may first arise in parents rather than children. Parents may unintentionally communicate these feelings to the child, thus intensifying the conflicting sexual feelings in the child. Taking a psychological/sociological perspective on incestous feelings, Nancy Chodorow maintains that:

> Sexual drives toward a child are common, particularly if there has been a gratifying preoedipal parent-child relationship which has strengthened parental love. Society does not approve these incestuous wishes, and for the most part a parent's superego requires their repression.[14]

I think it is safe to say that incestuous fantasies are common to both parent and child in the adolescent period. Social mores and prohibitions, the protective dynamics of the family group and fear of total social and economic collapse of the family are good insurance against the possibility of these fantasies being acted out.

Actual incest is usually the symptom or result, not the cause of a disturbed family order. To argue against the effectiveness of opposite-sex training on the basis of incestuous fears is to miss the important point that most daughters and sons increase their probabilities of incestuous fantasizing if the parent of the opposite sex is remote and unavailable to them.

It is quite possible to argue, as psychoanalyst Marjorie Leonard does, for the father's importance in the development of the daughter's heterosexual orientation. In a book, *The Reproduction of Mothering,* Nancy Chodorow explains:

> Leonard argues that the father's role is crucial to his daughter's development during her oedipal period and during preadolescence and early adolescence. She gives clinical examples of ways a father can be not there enough, which leads a girl to idealize her father and other men. . . . Fathers, Leonard argues, must be able to make themselves available. . . . Otherwise, she implied, a girl will not develop proper heterosexuality.[15]

Fathers can play a critical role in helping their daughters develop good sound feelings about femininity by explaining to them how men feel. Too often the whole subject of male or female sexuality is made a mystery to a child simply by the mystery and unavailability of the opposite-sex parent.

Mothers can help their sons in the necessary process of separation by being available to explain how women think and feel. By showing that she is knowledgeable and aware of some of the very sexual issues that her son is struggling with, a mother can demystify herself and also educate her son so that he will better be able to enter into healthy sexual relationships with other females.

As you are reading this, you are quite likely thinking to yourself: "How could I as a father broach the topic of sex to my daughter?" or "How would I as a mother talk to my son about sex?" I urge you to carry these questions over into possible answers that are comfortable to you. Try to fantasize just what kinds of discussions you *would* have with the child of the opposite sex, what kind of dialogue would occur. Each of you is capable of creating the right script for yourself.

Possibly most satisfying of all is the fact that the advantages of opposite-sex training work both ways —for child and parent. A mother who explains to her sons the process of menstruation, showing him what a sanitary napkin and a tampon look like, and explaining the connection with reproduction, has the opportunity of being on hand for a number of questions about menstruation and sex that the son would probably never ask his father.

Similarly, a father can instruct a daughter on the topics that relate to male sexuality. Since I firmly believe that sex should be put into the context of life, and presented as normal a function as eating and sleeping, it stands to reason that this point can best be made when both mothers and fathers make themselves available for supportively guiding their sons and daughters.

Some parents have asked me, "Should I give my son more instruction about sex than my daughter?" or "Should I keep some of the information I give to my daughter from my son?" My answer is categorically *no.* I fully believe that what you teach a girl about girls should be taught to boys and what you teach a boy about boys should be taught to girls. This will help to eliminate the guessing games that both males and females participate in when trying to understand the opposite sex.

The single parent, naturally, faces unique problems and challenges. I am often asked, "What about the single parent who has children of the opposite sex? Can he or she handle this responsibility alone?" My answer to that one is obvious. I have a friend who has been divorced for a number of years and who has raised three sons virtually by herself. They are all healthy heterosexuals with no apparent sex problems. When I questioned her about how she felt as the sole sex educator in the family, she said:

> When I first realized I was to be the one, and the only one, fully responsible for training my sons in sex education, I had no negative feelings at all.

There was no sense of panic or threat; in fact, I felt relieved that their father wouldn't be doing it, given all the hang-ups he has about sex. I couldn't articulate to myself just why this was at the time. I just felt "right" about it.

My friend has an intuitive recognition about what was positive and healthy in a mother's training of sons. Perhaps a number of other people, in both single-parent and two-parent families, have similar recognitions, but these are rarely acted upon because of inhibiting social and cultural expectations. In fact, however, parents of the opposite sex have the advantage of being able to transcend some of the traditional "blocks" and frustrations that plague parents in their attempt to educate children of the same sex.

Most parents have real problems in remaining objective when teaching their same-sex child about sex. They often suffer problems of identification and negative transference that make an open, free flow of communication virtually impossible. A mother who feels ambivalent about her role as a woman invariably communicates this emotion to her daughter, severely limiting possibilities of discussion. One teenage girl put it this way: "How can I be open with my mother when she is so uptight about her own sexuality?"[16]

Fathers who have conflicting feelings about women have enough trouble sorting out their own emotions, let alone succeeding in giving clear and precise definitions and answers to a son who is beginning to experience the same conflict. A fifteen-year-old boy reported that "I can't be open with them because they are not open with me. My dad got fixed last year, and while he was in bed recovering, he said he had the flu."[17]

Given these communication difficulties, single parents with children of the opposite sex should feel heartened rather than dismayed. While it is, of course, best to have both mothers and fathers involved, there are ways that the single parent of the opposite sex can be very effective in producing a change in the ways that children are trained in their sexuality.

When I have had the opportunity to speak to groups about the benefits of opposite-sex training, I invariably get the question: "What do I do if I am a single parent with a child of the same sex?" Good question. Obviously, not all situations are tailor-made for opposite-sex parenting. In single-parent homes where one parent has died, or where there has been an unfriendly divorce, communication between the child and his or her opposite-sex parent may be impossible.

When this is the case, it is a good idea to draw on the resources of either friends or family to find someone of the opposite sex with whom the *parent*—not necessarily the child—can communicate. For example, a man who is raising a son by himself might look for some guidance from his girl friend or sister to get some information about how she would feel if asked to communicate sexual values and information to her son. Similarly, a woman who is raising a daughter alone may ask a male friend to give her some advice on how he would feel discussing sexuality with his daughter. The parent can then take some of this information and create for him- or herself a comfortable way of expressing the views of the opposite sex to the same-sex child. By being aware of the values of opposite-sex parenting, we can find ways to incorporate some of them into our own life-style, even if it happens to be shared with a child of the same sex.

I would like to mention another major concern of many single parents: the question of how they should address their own sexual needs while living alone with their children. Once I spoke to a large group of widowed women, ranging in age from thirty to forty-five, a period of a woman's life when she is usually quite sexually active. Their single most overriding concern was how to accommodate their own sexual needs in the context of living with their minor children.

Two fundamental questions arose during this discussion: first, the women wanted to know how their personal sexual behavior would affect their children; second, they questioned their right to engage in sexual relations while they were unmarried and solely responsible for providing a good sexual model for their children.

Typically, these women reported that the way they were currently handling this issue was to ask their man to arrive well after the children were asleep, around midnight. They would then have sex until two or three o'clock in the morning, sleep, and get up at five or six o'clock so that the man could creep out of the house before the children awoke.

Two feelings result from this kind of situation: (1) guilt over deceiving the children; (2) sheer exhaustion from lack of sleep. Neither feeling is conducive to good communication with children or anyone else. I suggest to single parents that they be as open and available to their children about the subject of their own sexuality as they can.

No parent need deny himself or herself access to the opposite sex for the sake of the children. Children today are much more savvy about adult sexuality than ever before. If a parent establishes open lines of communication about his or her own and the child's sexuality at the appropriate developmental level, there should be no difficulty in the child's acceptance of the parental need for sex at a future date.

We can no longer perpetuate the myth of childhood and adolescent innocence. It died long ago. Anyone who is raising a child today will confirm that a whole host of problems stems from the constant exposure of children to the adult media. Children today hear, read, and observe ideas and situations that were simply unavailable to children twenty or thirty years ago. Children today are forced to deal with issues that were never even discussed in the past.

This prepares them for very early exposure to sexual information and material. We know that most children and adolescents do not get these from their parents. Where do they learn? If we turn once again to Aaron Hass's study on teenage sexuality, we find that most adolescents get their information about sexuality from pornography. Out of his large sampling, Hass found that 91 percent of the girls and 99 percent of the boys had had some experience with looking at sexy books or magazines.[18]

Unfortunately, pornography usually does not provide children with useful sexual values. Pornography does not help them learn that sex is a normal and healthy developmental experience. Nor does pornography provide a timetable for when the onset of sexual activity should occur. That responsibility for sexual guidance rests with the parents themselves.

If we were to project what a child who is brought up in the ways I have been describing would become as an adult, we could envision a person who would be comfortable with his or her own body, feel free in discussing sex with members of the same and the opposite sex, be able to maintain an exciting, fulfilling, and meaningful sexual relationship with a member of the opposite sex, and, if he or she chose to have children, to become a responsible and communicative parent in developing the children's training in sexuality.

I urge parents who find this method of guidance and education appealing to take a good look at where you now stand with your children. If you have teenage children who have been brought up to accept silence about sexuality, now is not the time to suddenly begin intense and open communications. This could be devastating for a teenager who has adjusted thoughts, feelings, attitudes, and behavior to the climate of silence that surrounds the topic of sexuality in the home.

The key to this kind of training is that it be a gradual and developmental process. It cannot simply be forced at one particular moment in a child's life. It is something that requires planning, homework, and careful, delicate execution. It should occur so that the child is almost unaware of it, just as he or she is unaware of beginning to be competent at tying shoes, dressing himself or herself, learning manners, or becoming accomplished on a musical instrument.

Parents who are starting late, perhaps with a child who is fourteen, can begin very slowly and gently to open up topics of discussion. They should not attempt to intervene directly in the child's exploration of sexuality if they have never intervened before. They should attempt, through loving probing and affectionate assurances of parental support and acceptance, to discover what their child needs and how they can best provide that child with fulfillment of those needs.

For parents who have young children, and for individuals who are contemplating having children, the world is all before you. You have every opportunity to help make your children healthy, happy, sexually aware, adjusted, and satisfied adolescents and adults —if you dare to take the risk that your children might, at least in this area, be better off than you were.

You can remain sensitive to where your child is in his or her development by looking closely at what questions are asked, what emotions the child expresses about his or her body, and what interest the child is taking in the opposite sex. With your own love and support, and with the framework of ideas presented in this chapter, you can begin to build a saner sexual world for your child and, perhaps, for us all.

9 Questions and Concerns

WHEN I address groups or appear on television, the audience asks questions and I am able to respond directly in person. The reader, after having read the rest of the book, may have similar questions, and so I have compiled a collection of questions most frequently asked. If the book fulfills its purpose, it will stimulate more questions, and I would consider this a very healthy response.

I hope that any questions left unanswered will open up new areas of research. I also hope they will open up new areas of dialogue and communication between sexual partners, professionals and patients, parents and children.

1. What about love? Where does love fit into all this information about sexual preferences?

In this book, we have been viewing sexuality as a more or less isolated experience. We have taken it out of the context of emotional commitment and avoided extensive discussion of the emotional dynamics that underlie sexual activity. I believe that sexual relations are intensified by love, but that love is not necessary for sexual gratification.

In attempting to address this question in my speaking engagements I frequently draw upon the analogy of eating a candle-lit dinner at an elegant restaurant. You can go by yourself or with a business colleague or casual acquaintance and have an enjoyable meal and a pleasurable experience. If, however, you go with someone you love, your enjoyment and pleasure is significantly enhanced.

A similar experience occurs with sex. You can masturbate or have sexual relations with a partner whom you find attractive and responsive and find the experience satisfying and enjoyable. The degree of pleasure and satisfaction is, however, greatly increased when you have sex with someone you love. Love is not an essential ingredient for sexual enjoyment and fulfillment. But when added to the sexual experience, love serves to enrich, enhance, and expand one's needs, desires, and satisfactions.

2. Why is a study like this important?

Among other reasons, the Kahn Study is important because, up to the present time, no information on the subject of female sexual preference has been available to professionals who treat female patients. I have spoken with a number of gynecologists, obstetricians, sex therapists, psychologists, psychiatrists, and male therapists who admit that they have no idea what concerns women have about their sexuality or what activities women prefer sexually.

It used to be that women had no medical resource to tap when trying to get answers about their sexuality. Now, more and more women go for their primary care to one physician, a gynecologist. As women become increasingly expressive about their questions and concerns, gynecologists need to become familiarized with issues that surround female sexuality.

The gynecologist, along with other professionals who find themselves treating women, can look to my study and to this book as a source which can provide them with information on the psychology and sexuality of their female patients.

Another reason why the study is important is that we now have information about both male and female sexual preferences that can be made available to both sexes in an effort to achieve better understanding and communications between them.

3. Would the results of the study change if it were given to different ethnic groups?

This is a good question, and I do not like to respond with a categorical yes or no because, quite frankly, I am not sure. I do think that the key to a good study is that it allows someone else to pick it up and use it, like a springboard, to move on to other levels. I feel that another researcher could do this with my study in attempting to determine different results based on the participation of different ethnic groups. My own hypothesis is that, for the reasons I described earlier, the results would be very similar.

4. How much difference does age make in the results of your study? Would older or younger participants respond differently?

I think that age does make some difference in an individual's response to the sexual themes, and the difference is generally related to the amount of sexual experience the individual has had. One of the reasons I used persons in the age group twenty-seven to forty-nine is that the vast amount of previous research in sexuality was done with college students who did not have a significant amount of mature sexual experience. I wanted to use persons who had greater sexual experience at more advanced age so that they would be better able to handle the alternatives and determine the priorities that the study demands.

I would anticipate that younger people who are just beginning to be sexually active would find more conventional thematic choices like *sexual intercourse, male on top of female,* as most stimulating.

5. Isn't your sample already biased because all your subjects volunteered and were, therefore, already especially interested in sex?

Yes, but that is inevitable. When doing sexual research there is no other choice but to use volunteers. A researcher cannot force someone to look at photographs or any other sexual media. This must be a voluntary act. I could hardly have marched into a convent, forced the nuns to look at sexual photographs, and asked them to rank them in terms of preferences.

6. Were the results of your study surprising?

I usually respond to this question with another: "Surprising to *whom?*" I have observed some people, women in particular, listen to the results of the study while nodding their heads in calm agreement and understanding, with no apparent surprise whatever. I have also watched people express shock when they learn the results. So, to this question, I would have to answer yes and no.

The major surprise of the study was that women are not very surprised by the male results and that males are quite surprised by the female results. The most dramatic surprise was that oral sex was preferred by both men and women as the most sexually stimulating activity—more stimulating than sexual intercourse.

There is a mystique that surrounds oral sex, and I think both sexes find it confusing. Oral sex is not a topic of conversation among many people, and this very silence contributes to the confusion. Women are probably most confused by oral sex because they almost never discuss it among themselves. While women are not surprised that males find fellatio the most favored form of sexual activity, many of them are surprised to find that other females find cunnilingus the most stimulating sexual activity. I know one mother and daughter who would be very surprised to hear that oral sex ranked first for both sexes because when the daughter asked the mother what oral sex was the mother replied: "Oh, that's when a man and woman get together and talk about sex."

7. I am sixty-two years old. My parents never said a word to me about sex. My husband and I have a very good sexual relationship. I didn't think it was necessary to teach my children about sex. Why should I?

When women or men ask me questions like this one, I assure them that I respect what was comfortable for them and what they consider to be their best choice. I do think, however, that a woman like this sixty-two-year-old grandmother is extremely fortunate in remaining happy in her relationship with her husband. The majority of people who grow up with this type of silence about sexuality are not so fortunate and do, at one time or another, experience difficulties in their sex lives.

Also, when this woman was growing up, *nobody* was talking about sex and certainly not where children might hear. When her children were growing up, more and more people were talking about sex. Now, as her grandchildren are growing up, everybody is talking about sex. As parents, we cannot assume that the world is static and that what was right or workable for us will be the same for our children. The parent of today who remains silent about sex can bet that his or her child is hearing about it from plenty of other sources.

8. Is sex really that important to a love relationship?

Yes, it is. Sex helps to make a relationship meaningful and whole, and, when it is negative or absent, leaves a void. Without satisfying sex, other parts of the relationship are not as good as they could be. When a couple finds sex loving and satisfying, problems like money and in-laws can be more agreeably surmounted. When sex is bad or absent, they may find that these and other problems are overwhelming and ultimately destructive to their relationship.

Most of us receive our primary form of nurturance from touching and physical contact with others. When this essential need fulfillment is denied, problems can result.

9. I have been married eighteen years, and my husband has never satisfied me sexually. Is there any way that, at this point, I can change our sexual relationship without hurting my husband?

Yes, there is. There are ways of telling a man that you have not been fully satisfied sexually without coming out and telling him that he's been a rotten lover for eighteen years. Contrary to some recent literature on the topic of sexuality, I believe that a man, particularly a man who is in an intimate relationship with a woman, is extremely concerned about his partner's satisfaction and would like to know if she is feeling frustrated.

Men may not verbalize this concern, particularly after a number of years when habits may have set in and expectations about sexual activities become somewhat rigid. Part of the problem is that women, because they feel they are responsible for pleasing the man, often fake orgasm. When this happens, the man obviously is going to feel that his partner is satisfied and that there is no problem.

Women can become more responsible in attempting to change a frustrating relationship into a fulfilling one by communicating to men what it is they want and need. The myth is that a man does not want to know and that a woman would crush and bruise the male ego, emasculate the man, or cause the man to hate women if she dared to express to him that she was not being satisfied.

This need not be true. There are ways in which a woman can express herself to a man without threatening or diminishing his ego or his sexual performance. She can present it in terms of trying to improve their sex lives to become mutually satisfying and fulfilling. That is one of the goals of this book: to open up doors that have remained closed too long. Hopefully it will provide openers to both men and women. Once we see what is on the other side, there will be no question that the risk has been worthwhile.

10. Is the solidarity of the family being threatened by all this new concern for open expression of sexuality?

Quite the contrary; this new concern can help to bring the family together. In the past the silence about sexuality threatened the family because nobody could communicate to anybody else about living issues that were vital to them. When we begin to open channels of communication on the topic of sexuality, we can provide members of a family with new ways of bonding together. If handled properly, discussions of sexuality can give to a family an additional bond that manifests itself in a sense of sharing values and strengthening family ties.

11. What can we do about what other people tell our children?

Very often children do get confused by false information from others about sex. We can't control everything our children see, hear and observe. That is why it is so very important to keep the lines of sexual communication open in the home. Children should feel comfortable in bringing back information they have obtained from others and sharing it with their parents so that any distortions can be cleared up. Parents can anticipate this by telling their children that they will be hearing a lot from others about sex that will sound new, strange, and unfamiliar. They can urge their children to come to them with this material so that parent and child together can decipher what is true and what is false and what is right and what is wrong. I firmly believe that parents should be the primary source of information on sexuality and that any new material should be communicated to the parent so that myths and falsifications do not disturb the child's healthy perspective on sexuality.

12. What about all the current fuss about female orgasms? Is this really important and shouldn't we just let nature take its own course?

I believe that orgasm is a very important dimension of a woman's sexuality. I think that for a woman to desire orgasm is healthy and normal. What disturbs me about the current emphasis on the absolute necessity of orgasm is the amount of anger that is expressed in some of the recent books on the subject. Women seem to be placing the blame for not having orgasms on their male partners. The achievement of orgasm is a responsibility that should be shared by both partners. A woman needs to understand her body well enough to know what kinds of stimulation will bring her to orgasm and to communicate this vital information to her partner. Individual women vary in the ways in which they can achieve sexual fulfillment. Some need clitoral stimulation, some may need to masturbate, some need to employ fantasy. Both the man and the woman should attempt to understand and communicate whatever the need is and should avoid placing blame on each other. When a woman begins to blame a man for her sexual frustration and unfulfillment, she usually builds up an excessive amount of internalized anger that produces chronic depression, ulcers, and spastic colons—not orgasms. The anger that is directed toward the opposite-sex partner results in hostility, distancing, and further misunderstanding, all of which causes additional sets of problems that do not serve to advance the relationship. Women and men should be able to comfortably tell each other what feels good. Women especially should not assume that men know exactly how and where to please them. Men need to be helped and told, not blamed and resented.

13. What is your opinion about allowing nudity in the home?

There are all sorts of contradictory and varying theories about this. Freudian therapists feel differently from behavior-modification therapists who feel differently from Gestalt therapists. I have my own views on the subject of nudity in the home. My views work for me and my family, but they may not work for others. I believe that when a child begins to actively notice opposite-sex body parts, it is time for the opposite-sex parent to begin to be more discreet about showing those parts. Other people argue that nudity is a natural and normal part of family life and that the breasts and genitals should be viewed as any other bodily part. I have heard people make good cases for this argument. I certainly would not advocate being unnatural about it to the extreme of screaming or running in panic if a child unexpectedly walks in on the opposite-sex parent in the nude. I do think that the reader should be aware of the various points of view and should discover his or her own comfort level in the family. To my knowledge, studies have never been done to determine the effects of nudity or nonnudity in the home environment. As there is no established right or wrong, each parent is responsible for becoming the authority within the family structure.

14. Isn't it true that male impotence is now more frequent due to the increasing aggressiveness of females?

I believe that females, especially younger ones, are becoming more aggressive in terms of asking for sexual stimulation and fulfillment. Males can respond in one of two ways. They can be threatened by it, as some men will, or they can be excited by it, as other men will. Female aggressiveness is an issue that men will have to work through, just as we all have to work through any period of change. I recently saw a cartoon that showed a female boss chasing a male subordinate around an office desk. Working women are now asking of males the favors that they used to be asked for if they wanted advancement. Men will just have to choose which side of the desk they want to be on.

15. Does this new female aggressiveness contribute to male homosexuality?

I have heard this opinion expressed. I would challenge this view, however, as a person's fundamental sexual orientation determines his choice of sexual partners, not particular circumstances of the society.

16. Do women with problems of sexual dysfunction experience problems in other areas? What is the cause and what is the effect?

The term sexual dysfunction, when applied to women, usually refers to a woman who is preorgasmic, that is, has not yet experienced orgasm. The term preorgasmic replaces words like *frigid* and *nonorgasmic*. All women are capable of experiencing orgasm, and those who have not yet done so need special help and guidance in understanding their bodies and their needs. Often when a woman is preorgasmic, she does have other problems. One of the most prevalent symptoms of preorgasmic women is depression. This can be remedied in psychotherapy if the dysfunction is related to the woman's earlier fears and anxieties about sex. Sometimes the problem is not psychological but physiological, and this can be remedied by treatment from a gynecologist or a sex therapist.

17. What about incest between brother and sister. I hear it is becoming more frequent, and I'm afraid to leave my son and daughter alone together for fear that they will have sex. What can I do about it?

I think that the issue of incest, especially between brother and sister, does occur much more than we are aware of. Some of this contact is merely natural curiosity, some is actually incestuous. Natural curiosity might include a brother and sister viewing the differences between their anatomical structures, whereas incestuous behavior might take the form of sexual stimulation through touching and manipulation of the genitals. At some point, children must be told that incest is wrong. This information can be put into the context of the law, in that society deems it illegal for brother and sister to marry. Parents can explain that the children of brother and sister could have physical abnormalities. If a child expresses love for a brother or sister, parents can explain that this kind of love is different from romantic love and that there are different types of love that occur in human relationships, some that include having sex and some that do not.

18. What do I do when my little girl stands at the toilet and tries to urinate like her brother?

Very often, particularly if a little girl has a brother, she will pretend that she has a penis. This usually comes from a sense that something is missing if she has had the opportunity to view her brother's possession of a penis. I always avoid using the term "penis envy." I think that parents, when they observe their little girls pretending to have a penis, can use this opportunity to explain that she is not missing anything, that she is simply built differently and with different bodily parts than her brother or boys. Parents can explain that girls have parts that are very special and important, even though they cannot be seen, and that these parts allow her to have a baby, which boys cannot.

19. Aren't there other themes that could be incorporated in the study?

This is a question that is very frequently asked. I can assure you that after completing the study numerous people approached me with a variety of suggested themes, the imaginative range of which confirms forever the validity of Yankee ingenuity. It would really not have been possible to include the entire selection of sexual activities available to us in the study.

20. How should a parent handle a child who asks to bring home from college a partner of the opposite sex?

As with so many issues associated with sexuality, there is no right and wrong answer for this question. Everything depends on the parents and on what they are comfortable with. The important thing is to be open and expressive about how you stand on the issue. If you cannot accept the idea of your child sleeping with his or her partner under your roof, then say so. There is no stigma to insisting on separate bedrooms, if that is what is necessary for your comfort. Parents should not feel guilty or old-fashioned if they themselves are not ready to accept this behavior in their home.

21. You discuss the importance of self-image. What do you do with a child who is actually unattractive, with a weight problem or a skin disorder, for example?

There is no absolute standard of physical attractiveness. I have known men who consider the models for a *Playboy* center fold as too thin. Parents should remember that they can really help in developing a child's self-image, in spite of what the child may see in the mirror. Children need positive, assuring, and loving feedback from parents, and when this need is fulfilled, a child who would win no beauty contests by external standards can be made to feel beautiful and lovable inside. We can all find some attractive features in our children, and we can emphasize these. I do think that the media projections of absolutely beautiful and "perfect" is unfair and harmful and that parents should take some responsibility in communicating to their children that not everyone can or should look like Charlie's Angels.

22. Don't you think things have gone just too far and that we are throwing our morals to the wind?

No. I view what is happening today as positive and productive. I don't deny that the rapid change in sexual attitudes and behavior is somewhat scary. Any change is. Behind this change, however, is a reexamination and reassessment of old habits and thoughts that is very healthy and growth-producing. I do not believe that this will end in the destruction of society or in the disintegration of morals. We will find new and better ways to cope with and accept the change.

Sexuality is a very significant and healthy part of our lives. We have spent many generations repressing and denying this all-important dimension of human life. When we begin to change our attitudes and challenge our old ways of thinking, we can see the pain that this repression and denial has caused. We also experience the pain that accompanies the growth that this new kind of thinking has fostered. Any period of growth carries with it some necessary and inevitable pain, and we must accept this discomfort as part of the growth process.

We are in a period of transition, and we should begin to develop some healthy respect for the difficulties that attend that transition. Things aren't automatically changed and accepted as "all right." The key issue here is that the acceptance and growth will occur at different rates in different people and that we understand and respect our own rate of growth as well as that of others.

Some of us will experience a cultural shock as we watch the new waves of sexuality pound upon the shores of our established attitudes and beliefs. Others of us will be more able and willing to flow with the times and the tide and gradually incorporate the new as more effective and comfortable than the old. Still others will plunge right in and directly confront the new as something that must be absorbed as a necessary part of life. The important point is that we don't overwhelm ourselves with the new growth and drown in our attempts to accept or reject it. We must understand where we are as individuals and how much new sexual material can be accommodated or communicated at one time.

Appendix

TABLES A and B represent the statistical breakdowns of my results. The figures in the right-hand columns are the *average* rating derived from the three photographs shown for each theme. These results are based on the 0–5 rating scale described earlier in the book. The figure on the left represents the rankings of the theme by preference. These tables enable you to evaluate the significance of my findings using a mathematical model.

STATISTICAL TABLE A
Female Mean Ratings for Each Photograph

Ranking Order	*Theme*	*Mean Totals of Sets A, B, C (Average Rating)*
1	Heterosexual cunnilingus: oral sex, male on female	3.50
2	Triad: two males and one female joined together and engaged in coitus and/or oral-genital activity	3.41
3	Heterosexual petting, both nude	3.28
4	Heterosexual intercourse, female on top of male	3.24
5	Heterosexual petting, both partially clad	3.11
6	Heterosexual intercourse, male on top of female	2.91
7	Sadomasochism, male on female	2.69
8	Nude male	2.45
9	Heterosexual fellatio: oral sex, female on male	2.37

STATISTICAL TABLE A (*continued*)

Ranking Order	*Theme*	*Mean Totals of Sets A, B, C (Average Rating)*
10	Male masturbation	2.14
11	Homosexual fellatio	1.91
12	Sadomasochism, female on male	1.87
13	Partially clad male	1.64
14	Homosexual cunnilingus	1.51
15	Nude female	1.48
16	Female masturbation	1.34
17	Homosexual petting, female	1.26
18	Partially clad female	1.18
19	Homosexual anal intercourse	1.01
	Total	2.23

STATISTICAL TABLE B
Male Mean Ratings for Each Photograph

Ranking Order	*Theme*	*Mean Total of Sets A, B, C Average Rating Order*
1	Heterosexual fellatio: oral sex, female on male	3.32
2	Nude female	3.16
3	Heterosexual intercourse, female on top of male	3.12
4	Heterosexual petting, both nude	3.09
5	Partially clad female	2.94

STATISTICAL TABLE B (*continued*)

Ranking Order	*Theme*	*Mean Total of Sets A, B, C (Average Rating)*
6	Triad: two males and one female joined together and engaged in coitus and/or oral-genital activity	2.89
7	Sadomasochism, female on male	2.78
8	Heterosexual cunnilingus: oral sex, male on female	2.76
9	Heterosexual intercourse, male on top of female	2.72
10	Heterosexual petting, both partially clad	2.59
11	Sadomasochism, male on female	2.48
12	Homosexual cunnilingus	2.35
13	Female masturbation	2.02
14	Homosexual petting, female	1.84
15	Homosexual fellatio	.46
16	Partially clad male	.35
17	Male masturbation	.32
18	Nude male	.24
19	Homosexual anal intercourse	.21
	Total	2.09

Table C provides a statistical comparison of male and female preferences. The columns headed "Female Mean Rating" and "Male Mean Rating" refer once again to the *average* rating derived from the three photographs shown for each theme. These results are based on the 0–5 scale already described. The columns headed "Ranking" refer to the preference rank for men or women achieved by the theme overall.

STATISTICAL TABLE C
A Comparison of Females' and Males' Preferences for Sexual Activity

Theme	Female Mean Rating	Female Ranking	Male Mean Rating	Male Ranking
Heterosexual cunnilingus: oral sex, male on female	3.50	1	2.76	8
Triad: two males and one female joined together and engaged in coitus and/or oral-genital activity	3.41	2	2.89	6
Heterosexual petting, both nude	3.28	3	2.09	4
Heterosexual intercourse, female on top of male	3.21	4	3.11	3
Heterosexual petting, both partially clad	3.11	5	2.59	10
Heterosexual intercourse, male on top of female	2.91	6	2.72	9
Sadomasochism, male on female	2.69	7	2.48	11
Nude male	2.45	8	.21	18
Heterosexual fellatio: oral sex, female on male	1.37	9	3.32	1
Male masturbation	2.14	10	.32	17
Homosexual fellatio	1.91	11	.46	15
Sadomasochism, female on male	1.87	12	2.78	7

Statistical Table C (*continued*)

Theme	*Rating Mean*	*Female Ranking*	*Mean Rating*	*Male Ranking*
Partially clad male	1.64	13	.35	16
Homosexual cunnilingus	1.51	14	1.35	12
Nude female	1.48	15	3.16	2
Female masturbation	1.34	16	2.02	13
Homosexual petting, female	1.26	17	1.84	14
Partially clad female	1.18	18	2.94	5
Homosexual anal intercourse	1.01	19	.21	19

Notes

Introduction

1. Sigmund Freud, "Femininity," in *New Introductory Lectures On Psychoanalysis* (London: Hogarth Press, 1953).
2. John Paul Brady and Eugene E. Levitt, "Sexual Preferences in Young Adult Males and Some Correlates," *Clinical Psychology*, 1965, pp. 348–54.
3. A.C. Kinsey, et al., *Sexual Behavior in the Human Female* (Philadelphia: W.B. Saunders, 1953).
4. See Helen Singer Kaplan, *The New Sex Therapy* (New York: Brunner/Mazel, 1974), and Lonnie Garfield Barbach, *For Yourself: The Fulfillment of Female Sexuality* (New York: Doubleday, 1975).

Chapter 1

1. Caryl Rivers, Rosalind Barnett, Grace Baruch, *Beyond Sugar & Spice: How Women Grow, Learn, and Thrive* (New York: G. P. Putnam's Sons, 1979), p. 102.
2. Laura S. Sidorowicz and G. Sparks Lunney, "Babies X Revisited," *Sex Roles*, vol. 6, no. 1 (February 1980), pp. 67–73.
3. For an educated and responsible treatment of prenatal sexuality see Hilary M. Lips and Nina Lee Colwill, "Sexual Differentiation and Gender Identity," in *The Psychology of Sex Differences* (New Jersey: Prentice-Hall, 1978), pp. 52–79.
4. Sigmund Freud, "Some Physical Consequences of the Anatomical Distinction Between the Sexes," in *Theories of Personality: Primary Sources and Research*, Ed. by Gardner Lindzey and Calvin S. Hall (New York: John Wiley & Sons, Inc., 1965), pp. 13–17.
5. Shere Hite, *The Hite Report* (New York: Dell, 1977).
6. Ibid., p. 70.
7. Leah Cahan Schaefer, *Women and Sex* (New York: Pantheon, 1973), p. 121.
8. Aaron Hass, *Teenage Sexuality* (New York: Macmillan, 1979), p. 86.

9. Ibid., p. 96.
10. Rivers et al., *Beyond Sugar & Spice*, p. 177.
11. Elizabeth Janeway, *Man's World, Woman's Place* (New York: Delta, 1972).
12. See Nechama Liss-Levinson, Emily Coleman, and Laura Brown, "A Program of Sexual Assertiveness Training for Women," *The Counseling Psychologist*, vol. 5, no. 4 (1975), pp. 74–78.
13. Elizabeth Douvan and Joseph Adelson, *The Adolescent Experience* (New York: John Wiley & Sons, 1966).
14. Hass, *Teenage Sexuality*, p. 75.
15. Catherine Chilman, *Adolescent Sexuality in a Changing American Society* (Washington, D.C.: U.S. Department of Health, Education and Welfare, 1979).
16. Margaret Mead, *Male and Female* (New York: William Morrow and Company, 1949).
17. Ibid., p. 175.
18. Barbara Seaman, *Free and Female: Sex Life of the Contemporary Woman* (New York: Coward, McCann and Geoghegan, 1972).
19. Anthony Pietropinto, and Jacqueline Simenauer, *Beyond the Male Myth* (New York: Signet, 1978).
20. Ibid., p. 52.
21. Ibid., p. 31.
22. William H. Masters and Virginia E. Johnson, *Human Sexual Inadequacy* (Boston: Little, Brown, 1970), pp. 99–100.
23. Douvan and Adelson, *Adolescent Experience*, p. 347.
24. Robert May, *Sex and Fantasy: Patterns of Male and Female Development* (New York: Norton, 1980), p. 140.
25. Leslie Farber, "He Said, She Said," in *Lying, Despair, Jealousy, Envy, Sex, Suicide, Drugs and the Good Life* (New York: Basic Books, 1976).

Chapter 2

1. Masters and Johnson, *Human Sexual Inadequacy*.
2. Nat Lehrman, *Masters and Johnson Explained* (Chicago: Playboy Press, 1970).

3. Erica Jong, *Fear of Flying* (New York: Signet, 1974), p. 154.
4. Nancy Friday, *My Secret Garden: Women's Sexual Fantasies* (New York: Trident, 1973).
5. Nancy Friday, *Forbidden Flowers: More Women's Sexual Fantasies* (New York: Pocket, 1975).
6. Hite, *The Hite Report.*
7. Karen Shanor, *The Fantasy Files* (New York: Dial, 1977).
8. Ibid., p. 4.
9. Carol Tavris and Susan Sadd, *The Redbook Report on Female Sexuality* (New York: Dell, 1978).
10. Ibid., p. 128.
11. May, *Sex and Fantasy.*
12. An interesting study that defines two general types of erotic literature is Leon A. Jakobovits, "Evaluational Reactions to Erotic Literature," *Psychological Reports,* 16 (1965) pp. 985–994.
13. Brady and Levitt, "Sexual Preferences," p. 347.
14. Ibid., p. 349.
15. See, for example, Jack D. Hain and Patrick H. Linton, "Physiological Response to Visual Sexual Stimuli," *Journal of Sex Research,* vol. 5, no. 4 (November, 1969), pp. 292–302; and Jakobovits, "Reactions to Erotic Literature," *Psychological Reports,* 16, pp. 985–994.

Chapter 4

1. Kinsey, et al., *Sexual Behavior in the Human Female.*
2. Marilyn French, *The Women's Room* (New York: Jove, 1978).
3. Ibid., p. 456.
4. Hite, *The Hite Report.*
5. Masters and Johnson, *Human Sexual Inadequacy.*
6. Vokmar Sigusch, Gunter Schmidt, Antje Reinfeld, and Ingeborg Wiedemann-Sutor, "Psychosexual Stimulation: Sex Differences," *Journal of Sex Research,* vol. 6, no. 1 (February, 1970), pp. 10–24.
7. Kinsey, et al., *Sexual Behavior in the Human Female.*
8. Carmen Kerr, "Feminist Sexual Therapy," *Issues in Radical Therapy,* vol. 3, no. 1 (Winter 1975), p. 7.

9. Nancy Friday, *Men in Love: Men's Sexual Fantasies, The Triumph of Love Over Rage* (New York: Delacorte, 1980).
10. Ibid.

Chapter 5

1. Kinsey documented that the missionary position was "the traditional position throughout European and American cultures" for both males and females. See Kinsey, et al., *Sexual Behavior in the Human Female,* p. 362.
2. Elizabeth McNeill, *9½ Weeks: A Love Story* (New York: Berkeley, 1978).
3. Kinsey, et al., *Sexual Behavior in the Human Female.*
4. Friday, *Men in Love.*
5. Hite, *The Hite Report.*

Chapter 6

1. Meredith Daneman, *A Chance to Sit Down* (New York: Doubleday, 1972).

Chapter 7

1. Nancy Friday, *My Mother, My Self* (New York: Delacorte, 1977).

Chapter 8

1. E. Roberts, D. Kline, and J. Gagnon, *Final Report: Family Life and Sexual Learning* (Project on Human Sexual Development, Inc., Population Education, Inc., 1978).
2. As quoted in William Hines, "Sex Education of Girls Termed Too Late," *Chicago-Sun Times,* August 28, 1979, p. 15.
3. As quoted in Laura Berman, "*Can Mother Deal With Daughter's Sex Life?,*" *Chicago Tribune,* August 19, 1979, p. 10.
4. Germaine Greer, *The Female Eunuch* (New York: McGraw-Hill, 1971).
5. Paula Weideger reports that in a response to a ques-

tionnaire, one woman discussed how her family celebrated a twelve-year-old's first menstruation by drinking wine, toasting her, and having her receive a bunch of wild flowers from her father. See her *Menstruation and Menopause* (New York: Knopf, 1976).
6. Ibid.
7. As quoted, in R. Lincoln, F. S. Jaffe, A. Ambrose, *11 Million Teenagers* (New York: Alan Guttmacher Institute, 1976).
8. Hass, *Teenage Sexuality*, p. 66.
9. As quoted in Berman, "Daughter's Sex Life."
10. Tavris and Sadd, *Redbook Report*, p. 22.
11. Hass, *Teenage Sexuality*, p. 168.
12. Ibid., p. 176.
13. Ibid., p. 166.
14. Nancy Chodorow, *The Reproduction of Mothering: Psychoanalysis and the Sociology of Gender* (Berkeley: University of California Press, 1978), p. 161.
15. Ibid., p. 118.
16. Hass, *Teenage Sexuality*, p. 170.
17. Ibid., p. 166.
18. Ibid., p. 154.

Index